Donated by Prison Alliance
Write us a letter & enroll in
our PA Bible Study today!
PO Box 97095 Raleigh NC 27624

MORE THAN A COINCIDENCE

IN OUR MIDST

SUSAN FISKUM HALL

ISBN 979-8-88644-155-0 (Paperback)
ISBN 979-8-88644-157-4 (Hardcover)
ISBN 979-8-88644-156-7 (Digital)

Copyright © 2023 Susan Fiskum Hall
All rights reserved
First Edition

Scripture taken from the New King James Version
Copyright 1982 by Thomas Nelson, Inc.
Used by permission

All rights reserved. No part of this publication may be reproduced, distributed, or transmitted in any form or by any means, including photocopying, recording, or other electronic or mechanical methods without the prior written permission of the publisher. For permission requests, solicit the publisher via the address below.

Covenant Books
11661 Hwy 707
Murrells Inlet, SC 29576
www.covenantbooks.com

This book is dedicated to my brother, David Lawrence Fiskum. If I could have chosen a brother, it would have been him. He not only put up with me, the older sister, but he is also always there for me, and when I ask him, he has the wisest advice ever. He never knows a stranger and is truly interested in others. He is the best!

Our parents left memories and a legacy as well. Our mother, Doris Virginia Fiskum, certainly was a gift. By her example, she showed what a giving heart was like. She gave us joy and comfort; she had a fabulous sense of humor and a great spirit, and she showed her unwavering faith in God even when she did not understand. Most of all, she gave us unconditional love. I would say she is the person who most influenced me by her spirit, example, and sense of humor.

Our father, Lawrence Fiskum, served our country during World War II. He initially served in the Office of Strategic Service (the forerunner of the CIA) until the day the war ended, and it was dissolved. My father then served in the Air Force. He was what I would call a patriot. He had the gift of foresight of so many major changes and warnings that would occur in the future even though he died in 1976. Many have already occurred or are happening now. Now I marvel as I see these things unfold in our country and around the world—what he predicted seemed not even possible. I admire his courage and fearlessness with what he did before I was even born. Not until after I was grown did I know a few things as he did not tell us much as military records were confidential. I knew he was a paratrooper who spoke the Norwegian language. I found out later he was in an OSS group that jumped into enemy territory and skied even at night. I cannot even imagine what these people did for our great United States. I have no idea of their missions but am trying to research what I can. I am in the process of trying to access the military records that are declassified but have not yet accomplished that.

My parents touched so many lives while they were here, and I owe them a gift of thanks.

Presented to: Luann
From: Susan
Date: Sept 2023

Susan

770 3562278
hall.susan1@gmail.com

INTRODUCTION

Ever since I can remember, I have known I wanted to write a book. I remember talking with my mother and saying if I did, it would be in the science fiction category because who would believe it! Little did I know that one day, I would write about situations and people that would be astonishing in so many ways. I just knew it was a "someday" dream, and that is all I knew. It was a faint glimmer in the back of my mind—a firefly of a dream with its light flickering on and off for many years.

I found myself in an unexpected job transition, and although not planned, it was on my youngest son Brian Winn's birthday that I made a decision to begin. As I began to write, I had to pinch myself—I could not believe I had arrived at that elusive "someday."

All this was due to the fact that during this job transition, as I was speaking with my friend, Dr. Anne Caffey, she asked me what I loved to do. When I responded that writing about some of the things that happened to me and sharing them with my three sons—Spence, Brett, and Brian Winn—would be fun, she suggested I do just that. So I began. The one of my friends, Millie Ross, suggested I ask others for stories of things that had happened to them that were unusual or unexplainable. I thought this was a great idea and took her advice. An amazing person I think of as a real-life angel of encouragement told me that people would be interested in reading what I had to share. As startling as this was for me to hear, I decided to begin with that end in mind. In conversations where my book came up and I told people what I was working on, people would volunteer their stories, and many agreed that I could use them in my book. Since I prayed originally that I only wanted the stories that God wanted, it was quite interesting what people agreed to share.

Just as I was close to nearing the end of this collection of stories, I began work as a relationship banker at a well-known bank and stayed there for over thirteen years. I have some stories from that time I will share that will be in a later volume. I never had the desire to go forward with the book after working all day. But my dream continued in the back of mind, and I knew I would go forward when it was the right time.

When God showed me in the most surprising way that it was time to retire from banking, I then knew it was the time to step out in faith and publish this book. Retiring from this job was a major and difficult decision. I have met so many wonderful people during my career. However, I knew it was time to start on the next chapter of my life.

God, however, never ceases to surprise me. One of our clients that I had met during the time I was working at the branch had told me he had exactly the same position as I did at the very same branch under a different manager several years back. After he left that position, he opened his own business. In addition, he and his wife also pastor a church, and their passion is spreading the gospel no matter where they are. They are both awesome, inspiring people, and when you are around them, you can feel the love of Jesus shining from both of them. I have attended their church service but had not seen them for a while. Although I had thought about letting them both know that I was retiring from the bank, I just had not yet done so.

On my very last day of my banking career, at about *two* minutes before we were to close the bank doors for the night, this client came into the bank to the teller line and then walked into my office. As I looked up in surprise and told him I could not believe he was my very last client on my very last day at the last two minutes of my banking career, he surprised me by saying he had not planned to come by. I told him I was retiring, and he prayed the most beautiful prayer for provision and blessings. I have told many people this story of how God ended my thirteen-year banking career in the most unexpected way. Although I knew, after much prayer, that I was doing the right thing by retiring, this awesome prayer was a breathtaking blessing. I am still amazed when I share this story with people. All I can say with astonishment is "Only God!" I knew this story was so important I wanted to share it in this book.

As soon as I retired, I also had a knowing that this was now the time to begin the process of publishing this book. So from the initial idea fifteen years ago—yes, fifteen long years until now, I knew it was time to finally get out of the boat. I am delighted to walk on water. I hope you will come along with me and enjoy the journey!

I would love to hear your comments. I can be found on Facebook under the title of the book, *More Than a Coincidence: In Our Midst*, or you can email me at contactsusan1000@gmail.com.

CHAPTER 1

Provision

Be anxious for nothing, but in everything by prayer and supplication, with thanksgiving, let your requests be made known to God. And the peace of God which surpasses all understanding, will guard your hearts and minds through Christ Jesus.
—Philippians 4:6–7

SUSAN FISKUM HALL

Dare You to Move
Anonymous
Atlanta, Georgia

My husband is an architect, and for the past seven years, times have been lean as we struggled to make ends meet. We had two sons in college and hefty tuition bills. After September 11, 2001, the work situation worsened, and my husband was laid off. We accumulated quite a lot of debt during this time and were trying to get back on our feet. My husband started his own architectural company until a permanent position became available.

During this time, the church we attended in Alpharetta, Georgia, took on a major building campaign called Dare You to Move. The pastor asked people to pledge to donate to a new church to be built at another location in Georgia and be part of the growth of the church. Although we already tithed 10 percent of our income, we decided to step out in faith and pledge $2,500 over and above our regular offerings over the next year 2004. We had no earthly idea how the money would arrive, or if it would at all, and decided we would trust in God.

One day, my husband received a surprise call from a colleague at another firm. A potential client had called needing the services of an architect to produce a concept design and rendering for a project. My colleague needed to charge more than this potential customer was able to pay but told the client he knew someone who might be able to help him for a lesser fee. This colleague then called my husband and asked if he would be willing to work on this project for $25,000. My husband, who wanted to jump up and down with joy, contained himself and agreed in his usual professional voice to do the work for this price. He told me the price was fair, but he would have charged even less due to the fact he needed work.

Three or four days later, we both realized the $2,500 we had pledged to the church for the building project was exactly 10 percent of the amount of this new architectural project! We both thanked God for providing the work and the ability to honor our church pledge. We now had enough money to pay our back taxes.

The next good news is my husband now has a full-time position with an architectural firm, and we have steady income to rely on at this time. We have again pledged another $2,500 for the church building fund for the year 2005. We again have no earthly idea where the money will come from, and I guess that is the point—no earthly idea. I can hardly wait for the end of this story!

Note from Susan

I have the end of the story. It happened again. After I had written this story, but before I had the final chapters ready to print, I was told the second pledge was met through an unexpected source of income, just as the first pledge. This has been a faith builder for this couple, and they are "cheerful givers." God has been faithful.

The Path to Atlanta
Mike Teston
Atlanta, Georgia

My family and I lived in Virginia, and I was on staff at a church. I didn't feel like I was in the right position, and stirrings of unrest kept fluttering in my soul. I felt like I was pushing myself to work every day and was void of any feeling of satisfaction or accomplishment. Still, it wasn't always easy to pick up and move, not when you have children in school, mortgage payments, and all the expenses that go along with everyday life.

I plugged away for several years, thinking and hoping that things would change at work. Well, things did not, and I remember one day talking to my wife and saying I felt like I was a square peg in a round hole. The time had come to make a change. With her support, I left the church and my staff position and took on a new job, a job so different from anything I had ever done before. I worked in the construction industry while looking for other work. Used to being in an office and attending to numerous challenges and returning home at the end of the day clean and tidy, I enjoyed the change of being outside and working with my hands. The work was very physical, and this extreme change renewed my spirit and gave me a new perspective. I took a tremendous salary cut during this time.

This transition lasted about a year when a position opened up at a church in Atlanta. This was my dream job because this new position utilized most of the skills and talents I enjoy most. The opportunity to work at a church that was changing lives in a dramatic fashion by leading people into a growing relationship with Christ excited me. I find it difficult to express how amazed I was this opportunity had become available and that I was accepted for the position. With my renewed spirit, I moved my family to our new Atlanta home. There was a time I could only imagine this job in my wildest dreams, and here I was living it. If I died tomorrow, I could only say how thankful I was to have such an opportunity at serving at this church.

During the long time I was in the transition, I relied heavily on the Bible verse in 1 Peter 5:6 that sustained me that long year: "Humble yourself, therefore, under the mighty hand of God that He may lift you up in due time." All I can say again and again is "Thank you, Father."

Note from Susan

Mike is on the staff at North Point Community Church in Alpharetta, Georgia, at the time this story is being written. When we find ourselves out of a job—and I am speaking to myself as well—if we are open to God's will and trust Him, He will make our path straight! I am very interested in this story as I have been in a similar position myself and know others who are as well. For me, it is the waiting and the unknown that are difficult. I know there is a reason—and sometimes that is the only thing I know—and since God is always there, I am continuing to trust in Him. His ways are not our ways!

Where There Is a Will, There Is an A!
Dorothy Traewick
Sandersville, Georgia

I am the baby of the family—the sixteenth child born to my mother. Fourteen of us lived to adulthood. Mom was forty-seven at the time of my birth, and my father was sixty years old. Can you imagine having children at that age?

My father had a rough childhood. His own mother put him out of the house at night, and he was only five years old. I remember him telling me he decided he would go to the white family that lived over a quarter mile from his house. He remembers passing by an open well, seeing the reflection of the moon and realizing he could have easily fallen in. He was fortunate to be taken in and reared by a white family, not something very common in those days for a black child. He lived his life as a sharecropper until 1939 when he was able to buy 378 acres of his very own to farm. This was quite an accomplishment. Although he wasn't allowed to go to school, one of the daughters in the family took it upon herself to teach him to read and write. He learned to read better than many who were in high school and excelled not only in reading but math as well. This helped in the excellent recordkeeping skills he needed for his farm.

I was born during the time when he and my mother owned the farm. I got used to hard work real quick. I remember at about four years of age, I would walk on my little legs to the spring to get water for the hands working in the field. As soon as I was able, I moved on to other chores. If crops needed picking, I did it. If cows needed milking I was there. Whatever I was told to do I did. I remember thinking, *I am not going to spend my life in the field. I want to become a teacher.* Now that I think about it, I am baffled how I even knew there was a possibility of another life or to even determine what I wanted to do at a very young age. I had many daydreams about running away. My next sister closest in age to me was five years older. At eighteen, she left home, and I was devastated. There I was, alone with only my parents. I missed her terribly. I even entertained thoughts about living out west—don't know how I came up with this idea either. We had no relatives in that part of the country. I sure didn't like my life. It was hard, and my father was domineering. My father died when I was only thirteen.

My mother was a wonderful Christian woman who read to me and gave me Bible story lessons. One of the lessons that stayed with me my entire life was to always do my best and, the most important of all, put God first.

Wanting to play the piano, in the worst way, I would pretend by tapping my fingers on the kitchen table. My mom began to pray she would be able to get a piano for me, and she saved every penny to accomplish this goal. In the meantime, she found someone who would teach me for fifty cents a lesson. After I had taken three lessons, my mother saved enough money to buy a piano for twenty dollars. But she could not afford to pay for more lessons. I was blessed with enough talent that I could play in church, and I was able to learn easily. I played mostly spiritual and gospel music, and I still love the piano.

When I was about fifteen or sixteen years old, I found a job outside the farm. I worked at a small restaurant in town from 11:00 AM to 11:00 PM for $1.35 per day! Even in those days, it was still a piddly amount. The restaurant was three and a half miles from town, and the owners picked me up and brought me home. They didn't allow me to eat from the restaurant during that entire time unless they deducted it from my pay. Generous people! One day, I found a dime on the table. I gave it to the owners—I didn't realize it was a tip for me. No surprise that she didn't give it to me.

In school, I studied like crazy and graduated fifth in my high school class in 1964. Consequently, I was eligible for a National Defense Loan of $544—enough for two quarters of schooling. I decided on Savannah State College, now known as Savannah State University, to pursue a degree in teaching—I still had my dream. I didn't have enough money for the application fee and almost gave up on going until one of my sisters lent me the money. This was a real adventure for me. I packed my brand-new white three-piece luggage set that my mom gave to me and boarded the Nancy Hanks train that traveled from Atlanta to Savannah and stopped in Tennille, Georgia, where I lived. I was excited and scared at the same time. I had fourteen dollars to my name, and a lot of prayer and courage. The train ticket cost $3.50, so all I had when I arrived at school was $10.50.

MORE THAN A COINCIDENCE

There in Savannah, far from home, I looked around at the campus in amazement—I had made it! However, when I went to my first class, the professor said we must purchase a textbook so we would have it the next day. The book was nine dollars, and all I had left was six dollars. Very upset, I went to the dorm, called my sister, and told her I was coming home. I had just enough for cab fare from the campus to the train. My wonderful sister said absolutely not! She told me to go back to the professor and tell him the money was on its way from my sister and I would have the book soon. I was afraid to go to this man, and instead, I borrowed the money from the librarian at the college who knew my oldest sister. I came so close to quitting, and I am thankful for my sister's wise words—she helped change my life. With her encouragement and a little borrowed money, my life was changed forever.

As part of the work study program, there were two jobs available—one in the library and one for the president of the college. That is how I ended up working for the president. I remember I had to borrow five dollars from him to go home on the train at Christmas because my salary of forty-one dollars per quarter was going to be sent in the mail, and I had no extra money until then. I continued to work, study like crazy, and was able to get additional loans so I could stay in school. It was not easy. From time to time, some of my brothers and sisters would send a little money when they could. My brother loaned me most of the money, and I repaid every penny of the loans I received from him and my sister. All along, I saw God providing my needs, sometimes just in time.

The four years passed quickly, and I was ecstatic to receive my degree in business education. I went on to graduate with a master's degree in mental retardation in 1976 from Georgia College in Milledgeville, Georgia. I was the only member of my family to receive a degree, and I began my teaching career with enthusiasm and excitement. I taught students and loved it every day for thirty-one years. And it's not over yet!

SUSAN FISKUM HALL

Note from Susan

As Dorothy told me this inspiring story of a young girl who had a dream and kept on until she reached it, I imagined she would be supportive of others who want to teach. She must have read my thoughts. Although I didn't say a word, in her next sentence she told me she does help others. I would have expected no less after hearing her story.

If this story doesn't inspire people to keep on with their dreams even under the most daunting circumstances, I just don't know what will. When I met Dorothy, I remember thinking, *Now, this is a person everyone would love to be around.* She was wearing a striking deep-blue suit and could have been on the cover of a magazine. It is astounding to even try to picture her as a little girl in the fields working hard and milking seven cows every night, a little girl who had a dream placed in her heart to help others and, with God's help, carried out that dream. After I heard her story, my thoughts were confirmed—she is beautiful not only on the outside but inside as well. Wouldn't you like to have a teacher with that background—someone who would encourage others because she knew what it was like to struggle to reach her potential? I know that is why she is such a great teacher. And as her mother taught her, she always put God first! Dorothy says she is the product of a praying mother.

Although retired from full-time teaching, Dorothy teaches Bible study for children and uses her talents to sing and play the piano in a nursing home ministry. She still finds time to work as a consultant for a cosmetic and skin care line in addition to working with a line of high fashion clothes and jewelry for women. She is truly an example of God's provision and direction.

Now I Know I Looked There!
Donna Jones
Middleburg, Florida

Simple and elegant, I had worn my favorite gold bracelet often for many years when one day I happened to notice it was gone. I remember with certainty putting it on my wrist early in that morning. I reviewed the day carefully, mentally retracing my steps. I remember removing groceries from the trunk of the car and had a feeling it might be there. Running out to the car and opening the trunk, I searched so thoroughly I could have applied for a job in airport screening. Nope, it just was nowhere to be found. I looked very carefully in all the nooks and crannies, even pulling up the mat and checking every square inch of that trunk.

I really liked this bracelet and prayed I would find it. About a week later, I searched the trunk again, and I found it. It was in a place I had searched before. I had left no stone unturned before, and now here it was. Some of you reading this may think I didn't look close enough, but I was there, and I know I did.

Sometime later, I lost the bracelet again, and for some unknown reason, I knew it was gone for good—and to this day, I have not found it.

Lost and Found Again
Susan E. Hall
Atlanta, Georgia

My brother David just told me a similar story just this very week. His wife had a unique and quite old sapphire ring her mother had given her, and she could not find it. This ring was near and dear to her, and Sheri looked everywhere. It was nowhere to be found. She continued to search, but she had no luck.

Sheri went out of town for a few days on business, and upon returning, she opened her makeup cabinet, the same one she opens all the time. There, in the very front of the shelf in the cabinet where no one could miss it, sat the ring. She was thrilled and ran to thank my brother for finding it. He said he would be glad to take credit; however, he knew nothing about it. He had been praying Sheri or he would find it. Sheri very seldom loses such things, and she had looked in this cabinet several times. I asked my brother if they had someone cleaning the house that could have found it and placed it in the cabinet. My brother said no one had been in the house but him.

Just When It Seemed Hopeless
Barbara Hughes
Alpharetta, Georgia

Although I didn't have to work, I had been thinking about going to school to become a dental hygienist. A career in that field would be very interesting to me because I enjoy the precise work and helping people. I began to pursue the degree at Perimeter College in Atlanta, Georgia. Before I could be accepted, I needed to take a remedial math class plus two algebra classes, and the time frame for completion was three quarters. I was thirty-eight years old and hadn't been in school in years, but that wasn't going to stop me. Although I used to do well in school in the past, these classes were quite a struggle. Undeterred, I dove into the books and took full advantage of the math learning lab with free math tutoring.

The Algebra 2 class was the last class required for acceptance. I was glad it would be over after the final exam the following Monday. I wanted to be fully prepared, and my plan was to visit the math tutor the Wednesday before the test. I had also promised to take my son and one of his friends to our lake house that weekend before. While they were having fun, I planned to study.

On Wednesday, I drove to the math lab and was crushed to find the note on the door stating the lab would be closed until the following Tuesday. I stood there for a few minutes just staring and rereading the message. Panic welled up in my heart, and my brain began scrambling for a solution. I couldn't believe it—I was sure I would not pass the test and would have to repeat the entire quarter, which would delay my acceptance into college. I decided I would still take my son and his friend to the lake house—after all, why ruin their weekend just because of my problem? Still, I was very disappointed, and trying hard not to be resentful took all of my strong resolve.

We drove out to the lake. At lunchtime, I found myself telling my son's friend what had happened with the lab. I was positive I would not pass the test on Monday, and I told him how difficult the class was for me and how hard I had been studying. God had a nice surprise for me. I discovered that my son's friend Paul was a math wiz, and he offered to help me.

Well, I passed the final. Based on my high GPA, I was honored to be listed in Who's Who in American Junior Colleges and am now a dental hygienist with an associate degree in dental hygiene. I received my degree at the age of forty-two.

I will always be thankful that God provided my own personal weekend tutor in Paul Fredette, now Dr. Paul Fredette. I have a career I love. I know God is in this, and I am thankful both to God and to Paul.

Note from Susan

I admire Barbara's persistence, and I know from personal experience how difficult it is to return to school at a later age. For those who don't enjoy going to the dentist, having a hygienist like Barbara, with her vivacious spirit, would make the experience almost pleasurable. I thank you for sharing this story to illustrate when we sometimes have no solution, God can show up in a surprising way!

CHAPTER 2

Protection

Because you have made the Lord, who is my refuge, even the Most High, your dwelling place, No evil shall befall you, Nor shall any plague come near your dwelling. For He shall give His angels charge over you, To keep you in all your ways.
—Psalm 91:9–11

Asleep at the Wheel
Anonymous
Atlanta, Georgia

I was driving home from work one afternoon, about four o'clock, on a traffic-filled highway in Atlanta when I began to get drowsy. I decided to take the next exit and get a caffeinated drink to keep me alert.

The next thing I knew, I was running over bumps in the road, the big ones that warn us we are too close to the side. I could feel my heart pounding in my chest, and my hands began to shake. I was almost skimming the guardrail and just about to hit a sign. I had been driving on the inside lane of traffic just seconds ago, and now I was on the outside lane and almost to an exit ramp.

I had fallen asleep at the wheel—never done that one before—and crossed four lanes of traffic. The bumping noises were what woke me. All of the cars in front and back of me must have seen what I was doing because there was not a car near me or even close. I was able to exit immediately and was so unnerved I made a trip to the police station to see if I had caused any accidents during my wild ride. Bet they don't have those kinds of visits from women drivers often. Fortunately, everyone in Atlanta was safe.

Luckily for others and me, I woke up in time to avert disaster. I don't recommend crossing four lanes while sleeping—it can be difficult while awake in Atlanta traffic. I know Someone was watching over me that day!

More Asleep at the Wheel
Anonymous
Orlando, Florida

Traveling from Charleston, West Virginia, into North Carolina has always been an easy road trip for me. I had driven it quite a few times before, and it was familiar territory. It takes about four hours to cover this distance.

Late on this very dark night, I got in my car and left Charleston. I felt all right until about two and a half hours of night driving. I began to feel my eyes get tired and my eyelids heavy. There was little traffic at two thirty in the morning, and the drive became monotonous. I should have heeded the yawns and monotony and pulled over to take a nap.

I took a nap all right as I discovered when something woke me up! To this day, I don't know why I woke up or even the exact moment I fell asleep. I was astounded to realize I had fallen asleep at the wheel. Because I recognized nothing and could not get my bearings, I took the time to backtrack and discovered I had driven about four miles while asleep on this road coming down from the mountains. I would not have believed this if I had not seen it for myself.

I knew Someone had to lead me; it wasn't possible. This is not a story I tell to many people unless they know me well. And if I heard this from someone else, I would not have believed it. However, it happened to me.

Damsel in Distress
Nikki Christiansen
Alpharetta, Georgia

I noticed a car I had never seen before, with a man behind the wheel, stopped in the middle of the road when I pulled into my subdivision. To get to my house, I had to drive around him. It was in the early sunny and chilly afternoon of February 2003, with a beautiful blue sky and the kind of weather that makes me glad I live in Atlanta. My home is in a nice suburban neighborhood of homes with their well-manicured lawns and winter flowers. I pulled into the driveway with my little preschool daughter, opened the garage door, but stopped my car in the driveway. My little girl ran into the house, closing the laundry door behind her.

I opened the back car door to take some things into the laundry room and was between my garage and the front of my car when a man approached me. Blocking my way, he stood between my car and me. At first, I didn't think much about his abrupt manner. When he reached into his pocket, I thought he was going to hand me a business card. He pulled out a gun and pointed it at me!

Help me, God, I prayed. When the man grabbed my arm and tried to pull me into the garage, the thought came to me to pretend to faint. I quickly fell to my knees and lay on the ground with my eyes shut, praying silently.

My neighbor, driving down the street, saw me fall. She had seen the man park his car and cut across another neighbor's yard and knew this was odd behavior. She started to wildly honk her horn, not realizing he had a gun and then screamed at the top of her lungs. When the man heard the commotion, he moved slowly to his car and took off. Workers at the end of our street heard all the noise and tried to find him by running down the street after him, but he jumped in his car and managed to get away.

Later we heard that someone in a car of similar description had tried to accost a young boy about eleven years old. One of our neighbors said that they had noticed a car with no hubcaps in the neighborhood a few days before and thought it could have been this same person.

I don't know why I pretended to faint. Where did the thought come from? How blessed I am that my watchful neighbor acted on her instincts and came to my rescue. If my daughter had been outside with me at the time, I could not have reacted that way. Even in the most difficult of situations, my little girl, my neighbor, and I were safe. I have no doubt in my mind that God protected us.

God's Protection
Anonymous
Orlando, Florida

I had a few roofing problems on my house, so I decided this was just the job for me—I could fix what needed to be done. Like most men, I knew I could take care of the problem. I am able to repair just about anything around our home.

Nearby were four chairs and a table on the deck. I placed the ladder against the house and climbed carefully onto the roof. I began my roof repair and was getting quite a bit of the work done when I started to lose my footing, and knew I was going to fall. As I began to waver back and forth, something caught me and steadied me so I could regain my balance. I had never experienced anything like this before.

As soon as I felt sure-footed, I finished my work, and when I came down the ladder, I noticed something looked different. Then I realized one of the chairs on the deck was in a different position. It was not by the table as it had been when I first climbed the ladder but had been placed close to the roof of the house.

You may think I was not paying attention, but you would be wrong. After my career at sea where everything had to be in its place, I notice all the details. No one had been there to rearrange this chair, at least no one that I could see! All this is to say I am grateful I did not have an accident that day, and I know I am never alone.

He Who Hesitates
Laszlo Suzter
Snellville, Georgia

I have a memory from a few years ago when I was twenty-five years old that will linger with me forever. I loved my shiny, sporty car and, even more, loved to drive fast. When I stopped at a red light, I would have my foot on the gas, ready to take off the split second the light turned green. I wouldn't glance around to see if anyone else was coming. I was always in a hurry even if I had nowhere special to go. Those fast takeoffs behind the wheel are exciting.

On this particular day, I stopped at a red light, waiting for it to turn green, and for some unknown reason, I didn't zip through the light as usual. I hesitated and still didn't look around. An eighteen-wheeler tractor-trailer rig seemed to appear out of nowhere and barreled through the intersection. If I had looked around, I would have seen it coming. Because I hesitated instead of taking off through the intersection in my usual manner, I lived to tell this story. I am convinced my car and I would have been no match for the fifty-three-foot tractor-trailer. I would not have known what hit me. That day was a great lesson for me. Yes, it was a very good day! I am eternally grateful.

He Who Hesitates Is Lost—Not This Time
Anonymous
Atlanta, Georgia

I had been out for the evening, and as I walked to my car to go home on a very dark night, I had an eerie feeling. There was no moonlight or strange shadows or unusual noises. As I looked all around me, there was nothing I could see, but my adrenaline kicked in, and I was on high alert. Looking around the parking lot and in the back seat of my car, I saw nothing unusual. Cautiously opening my car door, I got in and turned on the engine. Still this feeling persisted. I drove out of the parking lot and was about to pull onto the highway when something told me to wait, not to pull out yet. For some unknown reason, I listened to my inner voice, and I did wait for a few seconds. A car passed by me going in the same direction I would be driving in a few seconds. Then I slowly pulled out onto the highway and followed. As I continued on following several car lengths behind, this car went through the intersection under the green light. Right then, a car at the intersecting cross street failed to stop and ran the red light. In seconds, both cars smashed together in a mangled mess of steel. The sound of the impact rang in my ears. Then complete silence. None of the debris hit me or my car. In shock myself, and in the darkness with only my car lights to see by, I ran over to the cars. The driver of the car that caused the accident was a young teenage girl. I could see her distraught, tearful face, and my heart reached out to her. The woman who had been driving the car in front of me died upon impact.

Thirty years later, I still replay this scene in my mind and think about how a few seconds can impact our lives forever. I think about that young teenage driver and how difficult it must have been for her to live with the fact that because of a mistake she made, someone died. If I had not hesitated to pull out, that could have been me. I am so very thankful I heeded my inner warning.

MORE THAN A COINCIDENCE

Here Comes Sylvia
Sylvia Dore
Alpharetta, Georgia

I was driving at about forty miles per hour or perhaps a teensy bit more. The rain sheeted down, and traffic was heavy. I was traveling on Interstate 75 near Dallas, Texas, heading southbound during a time of heavy construction. There were three lanes on each side of the interstate. The fourth lane was in the process of being built, with tall concrete barricades lining the interstate for separation. So picture me traveling down the highway with high concrete barricades to my left. I was driving in the inside lane. I remember several hundred feet back I passed a fifty-three-foot tractor-trailer.

I felt my heart jump, and every nerve in my body became alert when I saw that a short distance in front of me, all the lanes were full of stopped cars in every single lane. I tried to slow down in time to avoid hitting them. As I stepped on the brake, my car began to hydroplane. (If you have ever had that experience, it is a real attention-getter.) I had no control of the car, and knowing I couldn't stop, I tried to prepare in a split second for a crash. I realized in just seconds I was about to be a story on the evening news!

My car took on a mind of its own. I did nothing as the car turned to the right, shot across three lanes of traffic without hitting anyone, zipped up the exit ramp, and stopped right in the middle of it. *Holy cow*, I thought as I shook from fright. I knew I was in no condition to drive. I don't know how I had the presence of mind to think at all. I backed up a short distance on the ramp and pulled to the side of the road, out of the way of traffic.

As soon as I was safe, I breathed a sigh of relief and began shaking. Perspiration dotted by forehead, and I could hear the wild thumping of my heart. My hands shook as I gripped the steering wheel. My eyes widened as I watched from my car. I saw the tractor-trailer I passed earlier headed up this same ramp. Whether he would have been able to stop fast enough to avoid hitting my stopped car if I hadn't moved out of the middle of the ramp is something I still don't know. What I do know is that I wasn't the one who changed the direction of the car that propelled me across three lanes of traffic to stop in the middle of the exit ramp. This maneuver prevented me from crashing into the traffic stopped in front of me. I know this was God's way of protecting others and me.

I can still picture the man in the tractor-trailer. A truck driver sitting high in his cab has a very clear view of the road. I can only imagine his face as he saw me hydroplane across three lanes, head onto the exit ramp, and then back up to pull to the side of the ramp, out of the way! Jeff Gordon, watch out—you have competition!

Note from Susan

For those of you who aren't racing fans, Jeff Gordon, #24, is a world-famous NASCAR superstar.

Just Enough Light
Susan E. Hall
Atlanta, Georgia

One of my dearest and longtime friends went back to school later in life and graduated from college with honors. My friends and I were thrilled for her and wanted to celebrate her hard work. I was one of the people in attendance at her graduation. I didn't live in the town anymore, so I took the two-hour drive back to Dade City, Florida. After the graduation, we celebrated at her house. I left her home to stay at a motel about ten miles away just as it was getting dark. I remembered there were lights along the highway I would travel. This was important, as I knew I only had one headlight. The casing for the other headlight had burnt when someone installed it incorrectly. I had ordered a new one, but it had not yet arrived.

It was almost dark, and I decided I'd better get on my way. It seemed to get dark rather quickly, but the lights along the highway gave me a sense of security until the lights suddenly ended. I had traveled that highway many times before but never noticed the lighting because I could always see with headlights. Only one headlight made a huge difference. In a second, I realized my other headlight had gone out. Now I had only the parking lights!

I leaned forward with panic and adrenaline flowing, and straining my eyes, I looked for a place to pull over, but with such little light, I could not see where it would be safe. (If you have ever hit a patch of dense fog or blinding rain, you are familiar with the feeling.)

In a few seconds, a car appeared almost on my bumper out of nowhere. With the glow of these headlights, I could see a very short distance in front of me. I slowed down to almost twenty-five or thirty miles per hour, hoping there was nothing in front of me and the road was straight. Although it was hard to judge, my visibility could not have been more than fifty feet. I remember thinking how wonderful it was I could see this far. My eyes almost hurt as I continued to look for a place where I could pull off the road. I knew this car would pass me any second. Then the blue lights came on! This was the only time in my life I have been *delighted* to see a policeman—so delighted I could have jumped for joy.

I found a safe spot to pull over, and the officer came to my window. I told him how happy I was to see him. I felt like hugging him but decided to keep my arms to myself.

I told him about the burnt casing, and he asked to look under the hood to see for himself. When he came back to the window, I said the other light had just burned out. He told me if my lights go out again to switch to high beams. In my panic I hadn't even thought of that. The first thing that entered my mind was that was great information, so I could still drive instead of having my car towed that night.

The officer saw my car as he was driving in the opposite direction. He thought I had been drinking—common for people who drive around with no lights. Thank heavens I hadn't anything to drink. I didn't need a visit to jail. He gave me no ticket and watched me carefully as I pulled back out on the highway with my high beams on.

I don't remember the officer's name, but this event took place in Dade City, Florida, in the mid-nineties. I would like to thank him for shining light on my path—just enough light so I could see.

Now many of you reading this may think this was just a coincidence. It was not. I have many instances in my life where I had just enough light for the next step (writing this book is a good example), and I have thought of that night many times with amazement. When I get discouraged, I try to remember that when I need it most, there is someone or an answer or an amazing "coincidence." Except I know that it is more than coincidence, and I will have just enough light shining for my next step!

More Than a Tractor-Trailer
Fran Stewart
Lawrenceville, Georgia

After living twenty-six years in Vermont, I moved to Georgia and didn't know my way around. I found a job about thirty miles from my home and drove on a major artery every day going to and from work.

While I lived in Vermont, I had become aware of the importance of platelet donation because a young child I knew became sick and needed transfusions. Wanting to help others, I had been involved in this donation, called pheresis, for about ten years. I was scheduled to make a donation in Atlanta and scheduled an appointment after work in Atlanta. I remember I was very tired from working a stressful day.

To make the donation, the donor is hooked up to a machine, and the blood is drawn out, the platelets removed, and the blood reenters the body. Although I had done this process more times than I can count, for the first time, my body reacted to the anticoagulant that was given to me. At the time, I didn't know what was happening. I felt that an elephant had lumbered into the room to sit on my chest. The pain was excruciating. Unable to talk, the nurses saw my face laced with fear and pain and knew by my labored breathing I was in trouble. In seconds, they removed the needles and did everything to save my life. Later, I found out I had been going into anaphylactic shock. The nurses kept me at the donation center under their careful monitoring for several hours and did not want me to leave. The head nurse told me she was within thirty seconds of calling 911 if my pain and breathing had not improved.

MORE THAN A COINCIDENCE

Although I looked calm outside, inside I felt panic. The nurses wanted me to call a friend to drive me home, but I knew few people in my new city and no one who was close by. I worked about thirty miles from my home, and the thought of calling someone to drive me home and then have someone return to get my car seemed impossible. My feelings of loneliness and despair overwhelmed me in my new city. The nurses had no legal way to keep me and did *everything* they could to talk me out of leaving by myself. Their talk fell on deaf ears. I was getting out of there, so against their numerous protests, I left by myself.

Feeling weak and jittery, I struggled to walk to my car so I could drive home. I began driving on 85 in the right-hand lane. Anyone who is familiar with Atlanta knows 85 is a major artery. By this time, it was late at night, and if this wasn't enough, it was raining buckets. This was the good part! In a few moments, I began to shake uncontrollably, my eyes wouldn't focus, and I strained my eyes, attempting to focus on the road. I didn't want to take any of the exits I was passing, as I was not familiar with Atlanta as of yet and thought I might be in a worse situation if I got lost.

I remember grabbing the steering wheel and yelling through the hot tears streaming down my face, "God, I need help." Panic was overtaking me; I knew I was going to die. I never experienced such uncontrolled terror until this moment. Seconds later, a white eighteen-wheeler pulled up on my left, eased in front of me, and slowed down. My eyes locked onto the white square back of the truck, and its red taillights were like a homing beacon. As if on automatic pilot, I followed about a car length behind—much closer than I would normally follow such a large vehicle.

The truck never changed lanes. This is impossible on 85 where the right-hand lane frequently becomes an exit-only lane. I never had to hit the brakes, and no one cut in between us. I couldn't think for the next thirty miles as I continued straining my eyes to focus on following the taillights. When I saw my exit to my right side, I breathed a sigh of relief and exited. The truck continued driving north on 85.

The moment I was in the exit lane, I looked to my left so I could wave to the driver. There were other cars, but there was no tractor-trailer. He was nowhere—he simply disappeared. "He is gone," I remember saying to myself with disbelief. Looking again, I could not believe what had happened.

At this point, I was about one mile from my home. I made it home with no red lights to stop me. Exhausted, I fell into bed. As I lay there, I remember thinking there were no markings on the truck, not any signage or even those little signs on the back that say, "Is my driving safe? Call 1-800-xxxxxxx."

I called in to work the next day to say I would not be in. I told my supervisor what happened, and she said she would have been glad to take me home. It had never dawned on me to call her. I spent the next three days in bed until my system recovered.

When I felt alone and helpless, God sent his angels in the form of a white eighteen-wheeler tractor-trailer to guide me safely home. And I now have a dramatic event to remember for the rest of my life, an event that was so amazing; I have no doubt that I am never alone.

Note from Susan

When Fran first told me this story, she told me it wasn't until I sent her the sample of her story to read that she realized how she never had to change lanes on 85 in the right lane going north, which again is impossible. Anyone who is familiar with Atlanta can attest to the fact that the right-hand lanes end from time to time as they turn into exit-only lanes.

Fran has shared another story in this book "My Hard-Earned Lesson of the Heart." Be sure to read it.

Mysterious Music
Michele Pirkle
Cartersville, Georgia

Working in a beauty shop in Peachtree Corners, I remember thinking about one of my clients. The year was 1998, and she lived with her husband in Dunwoody, Georgia. This is what she told me.

Turning in for the evening, the couple went to sleep at their home without a care in the world.

Early morning came, and the woman was awakened by beautiful music outside. Just barely able to open her eyes, her curiosity got her out of bed, and she went to the window and opened the curtains. The music continued to play even louder—she had not been dreaming. Then her husband woke up and, at his wife's insistence, joined her at the window.

As soon as he stood beside his wife, they heard a loud noise at the same time a tree crashed through the roof. It landed on the bed where they had been sleeping moments before. Had they still been in bed, they said they would have been killed.

The couple never knew where the music came from. They believe God sent the music to warn them and protect them just in time. Sounds like it was heaven-sent.

No, Not That One!
Susan E. Hall
Atlanta, Georgia

Many years ago—oh, all right, many, many years ago—when I was about five years old, my mother went to the hospital for several days to remove the varicose veins from both of her legs. This was quite a serious operation back then. The veins were removed by incision, and my mother had to recuperate for quite a few days in the hospital. I remember her legs were encased in heavy bandages.

When I was grown, she told me about her experience. She said during the operation, the doctors removed the first vein. However, when the doctors were getting ready to remove the main vein from the second leg, she had trouble breathing, so they stopped the operation and left that vein in the leg.

Years later, when she was having bypass surgery, the surgeon needed a vein for the operation—guess which one. My mother knew that was not an accident. God knew just what He was doing long ago, and He was there with her that day.

Slow Down, Deer
Laszlo Suzter
Lawrenceville, Georgia

This was a life-changing event for me. You might have experienced similar circumstances in your life as well.

I was riding my motorcycle through the mountains on a beautiful sunny day, enjoying the scenery and the feeling of freedom with the cool wind blowing on my face. Most of the time, I pay little attention to the speed limit signs posted at thirty-five miles or less per hour. Eighty or so miles per hour is much more exhilarating. Hey, I am young, what can happen to me?

For some reason on this particular day, I slowed down to about fifty miles per hour. Before I knew it, a deer dashed across my path. Deer don't look both ways before they cross a street. If I had been driving as fast as I usually do, I am sure I would have collided with the deer. It wouldn't have been a good day for either of us. To this day, I wonder what caused me to slow down. Whatever the reason, I am grateful I lived to tell this story.

The Train, the Train
Scott Carey
Hoover, Alabama

It was 1985, and I was a young lad of twelve. My eight-year-old sister and I were riding with my aunt in her two-door car. My sister sat in the front, and I sat in the back. I remember there was something wrong with the front seat; it would not stay up. My aunt wedged a stick between the door and the doorjamb so the seat would not fall down.

My aunt was stopped on the railroad track when the crossing gate arm came down. There were cars behind her, and she couldn't go forward or back without crashing through the gates. Not knowing what to do, she panicked and jumped out of the car, leaving the driver's side door open. My sister opened the passenger door of the car and also jumped out. I tried to get out but couldn't move the seat because of the stick keeping it in place. I had never felt such fear in my young life as at this moment. With my heart beating as fast as it could, adrenaline pumping through my body, and my head sticking out the back window, I could hear the roar of the engine and smell the fumes. I was paralyzed with fear as the approaching train barreled down the tracks. I could smell the burning rubber and the screeching of the brakes as the engineer tried to stop the train. I screamed at the top of my lungs. My sister ran back and pulled me out on the driver's side. I slipped on the wet grass but did not fall. When I looked up, I was close enough to see the engineer of the train; he was wearing sunglasses and had a mustache.

To this day, I am astounded we had the time to clear the train. My aunt pushed us down so we would not see the crash. The car flew into the air when the train hit it; we heard the deafening noise, and none of the debris landed on us. It was totaled into a mangled piece of steel and was barely recognizable. I remember wishing I had seen the impact—it would have been exciting. Most young boys are fascinated with trains, and I was no exception. At my young age, I had no idea how close we came to being smashed until days later.

It took the engineer some time to stop the train. We could see him from the accident site as he ran back to us in terror. He was dripping with perspiration, he was out of breath, and his eyes were as big as saucers and brimming with fear. He was sure someone had been killed. He saw us run across the tracks, saw me slip but not fall, and saw someone else in the back seat of the car as the train hit. We assured him we were fine. I am convinced that Someone protected us that day, someone else right beside me, someone I didn't see.

The accident report stated the train was going seventy miles per hour upon impact. My uncle, who is also a train engineer, knew the engineer driving this train. He said this man went in for counseling after this happened. The accident was even more traumatic because of the fact that he did see someone in the car after we ran from it.

I know God is with me even when I don't see physical evidence. Knowing this has made my life easier—I trust He will see me through whatever comes my way, no matter what it is.

SUSAN FISKUM HALL

The Unseen Hero
Donna Watson
Marietta, Georgia

The day looked to me like so many Georgia days—the weather was bright and breezy, and I didn't think beyond the fact that it was good for driving. My husband, Phil, would be on the road again, driving in his fifty-three-foot tractor-trailer in South Georgia near the Hazlehurst area.

As he later told me, the morning began uneventfully—a good thing for a driver. The conditions were fine, and he took off just at daybreak. He has been driving for years, and it is something he could almost do in his sleep. As he traveled, another trucker was behind him traveling the same route. As my husband approached a curve, he tried to turn the wheel, but the wheel didn't respond at all. Used to handling many difficult situations, he calmly grabbed the wheel and forcibly jerked it. He then heard something no one ever wants to hear—a loud pop. He hung on to the steering wheel as the entire tractor-trailer shot across the road and landed in a dry ditch on its side. The driver's side door was now above Phil's head, and he was dazed and confused.

The other tractor-trailer driver, behind Phil for the last ten miles, jumped out of his truck. This young man, about five feet, ten inches and of slender build, scampered up the side of the truck. These trucks are huge tipped over on their side (about eight feet from the ground), so can you picture this man swinging himself up and then opening the driver's side door? Now remember, the cab of the truck is on its side, and he is now about eight feet from the ground. He has to open the door straight up, which takes much more strength than when the truck is upright. The man yelled to Phil to get out because the truck was going to catch on fire any second. Phil simply stared at the man. While smoke swirled through the compartment, he tried to move and realized his left hand was practically useless, limp as a rag doll. It had been damaged as it rammed through the windshield when the truck tipped. With blood dripping down his arm and shards of glass in his arm, he tried moving it again. Nothing happened.

MORE THAN A COINCIDENCE

Phil's rescuer got on his knees on the top of the truck and started trying to pull Phil out of the truck. My husband is a big man—about six feet, three inches and 220 pounds—so the rescuer was no match for him, but somehow this fellow got Phil upright in the cab. At this point, Phil realized that his right foot was stuck between the gearshift and the engine mount.

My husband's worst fear has always been about being trapped in a truck, and here it was happening! He pulled and pulled with all his strength, but the foot stayed tight. Then he distinctly felt someone jiggle his foot. After several movements, it was released, and he was able to pull it loose. The man on top again pulled Phil and dragged him out of the cab and up on top of the truck. Keep in mind that both men were eight feet from the ground. My husband was covered in blood, and it was dripping everywhere. Both were in critical danger, as the truck could explode at any second. When Phil was on top of the cab, right before he jumped to the ground, he looked at his mangled hand. As a matter of fact, it was mangled almost to his elbow, and he was thinking about how he would have to get prosthesis. Moving as quickly as they could and dripping with blood and perspiration, both men jumped at the same time.

Now both of them were only three or four steps away from the truck when the flames engulfed the vehicle. Phil looked around for the person who released his foot and realized it was just the two of them—at this point, there was no one else around. Anyone who would have been there to release Phil's foot would have still been there. It had only been a few seconds. This person would have had to crawl on his stomach under the truck and reach his hand up to where Phil's foot was stuck. Anyone who would have done that would have at least stayed to be sure Phil got out and called 911.

There is a happy ending to this story. My husband, weak and bleeding, was taken to the hospital with severe damage to his left hand—he lost half of his hand. After surgery, the doctor told him he would never use it again or be able to drive a tractor-trailer. Wrong thing to say to my husband. This is not a man who gives up. He made a test-drive six months later and went on to drive his tractor-trailer full-time for another three years.

We know that "someone" released Phil's foot—as a matter of fact, we think his guardian angels must rotate shifts because they are on call so much of the time.

Note from Susan

I could hear the admiration in Donna's voice as she told this story of how proud she is of her husband who would not give up.

Note to doctors—telling patients they will never be able to do something may not be true because sometimes God has other plans.

Say What?
David Fiskum
Orlando, Florida

In November 2004, I was working in my home office into the night, and I decided around midnight to turn in. My wife was asleep. Except for the cat, I was the only one awake in the house. The only sound to be heard was the Corvette clock ticking away in the room. As I turned off the computer, I felt an icy chill envelop me. At the same moment, I heard a voice. I almost jumped out of my skin! I can't remember the exact words, but "it" said something to the effect that everything would be all right. I looked around and said, "What?" and the voice repeated itself. There was no one else; I was standing in the room all alone. I need to add I am in my fifties, and up to this point, I had never heard voices, nor was Jack Daniels involved.

It took a long while to get to sleep that night. I kept wondering what "it" meant about everything being all right. The next day, I woke up at daybreak. My plan for the day included taking my nephew's classic Corvette to the car show in Daytona, Florida, in hopes of finding a buyer. I love Corvettes, and I looked forward to the day. This garnet (Florida State garnet color, I might add) with its convertible top is a classic beauty. I smiled as we traveled down the interstate in search of its new owner.

The drive took about an hour, and driving was fun—the day was sunny, and the temperature was about seventy degrees. It could not have been a better day for a car show. Driving about fifty-five miles per hour, I had almost reached the exit when I stepped on the brakes again and again and realized that they were not working. I felt very calm as I managed to get the car over to the side of the interstate without hitting anyone or damaging the car in any way. On this older '66 model, with a single brake master cylinder, immediately losing all braking power was not part of my plan! The car rested on the slippery, grassy embankment, and its tires seized the morning grass wet with dew. If the brakes had failed a little later, someone else might have been test-driving the car in heavy traffic and caused an accident. I could have been driving through the town and caused serious injury or worse.

This is the first and only audible voice of assurance that I have experienced in all my fifty years. In retrospect, I liked knowing that whatever was about to happen would turn out well. Thank you very much!

Needless to say, the car didn't make it to the show that day. The brakes were repaired, and I found a new buyer not long after. And I know who protected me that special day!

Note from Susan

This is a story from my brother, and I have to say nothing like an audible voice has ever happened to him until this time.

Too Close for Comfort
Anonymous
Atlanta, Georgia

After spending several hours shopping, I gathered up my packages and went to my car. I had shopped till I dropped, well, almost. Tired and anxious to go home, I started the car and pulled into the exit lane in the shopping center. I noticed there was one car in front of me. When the light turned green, the car in front of me turned left. Instead of pulling out immediately, for some unknown reason, I hesitated. In the next few seconds, a car coming the other direction ran the red light and crossed in front of me. If I had pulled out immediately, this car would have hit me.

When I got over my surprise, I realized that when someone runs a red light, the first person crossing at the green light is usually the one in danger, not the second one. I was the second car.

I saw the woman's startled face as she flew by me, and I understood that she didn't even know there was a light until she had run through it. This was a new stoplight, and it had not been at this location for long. My hesitation saved my life and hers as well! I think of this near miss many times and know God spared us both.

Who Says Cutting the Grass Can't Be Exciting?
Barbara Hughes
Alpharetta, Georgia

Our vacation home on a serene lake north of Atlanta was an hour away from our primary residence. This lake house was on the market, and my husband decided he would drive up there to cut the grass. When he asked me if I would like to ride with him, I hesitated. There wasn't much to do except watch him cut the grass and get caught up with my reading. As a rule, watching the grass grow or being cut doesn't turn into a race for life, but this turned out to be a day we will both remember for a lifetime.

As I sat outside on this bright, sunny day reading my book, I looked up to see my husband waving his arms madly, jumping around, and screaming. He had accidentally mowed over a beehive, and hundreds of bees swarmed over him, stinging him hundreds of times. Still waving his arms and jumping around, he dashed into the house to try to wash them off in the shower, and since he had no other clothes with him, he grabbed the same clothes and threw them on. All this took place in just a few minutes, and it is possible there were still a few bees tucked away in his clothes.

We both ran to the car. Although he always drove, this time he asked me to drive him to the nearest hospital. I looked over at him, and in just a few seconds, he had passed out. We had not gone very far. Rather than go to the hospital, I made a quick decision to drive to the nearby country convenience store frequented by many of the local fireman and rescue personnel. With tires screeching, I pulled in the parking lot and ran into the store. As the EMTs were being called, a nurse who happened to be at the store dashed over to help me and stayed with me when my husband was hooked up to oxygen. She even came with me when my husband was transported to the hospital by ambulance. This quick treatment saved his life.

What was it that made me accompany my husband that day to watch him cut the grass—that inner voice I listened to? Had my husband been alone, he would have driven and then passed out. He might have died from shock or the car accident that could have occurred. Others could have been involved in the accident as well.

I am so thankful today I was there with my husband and for the nurse who was such an angel of mercy—there at a country convenience store at the right time to help when we needed her most!

CHAPTER 3

Blessings

Blessings are on the head of the righteous, But violence covers the mouth of the wicked. The memory of the righteous is blessed, But the name of the wicked will rot. The wise in heart will receive commands, But a prating fool will fall. He who walked with integrity walks securely But he who perverts his ways will become known.
—Proverbs 10:6–9

MORE THAN A COINCIDENCE

An Unasked For Blessing for the New House
Millie Ross
Gulf Shores, Alabama

During the summer of 2004, I decided it was time for me to think about moving from my Atlanta home to a home near the gulf. My brother and sister-in-law and family would be retiring to this beautiful beach area near the Florida-Alabama border, and I wanted to be near them as well. After numerous trips to Gulf Shores, Alabama, I found the home I wanted to buy. Between the times I signed the agreement to purchase my new house and the actual closing of the property (within a three-week period), there were three hurricanes that plagued the south that summer, and what a summer it was! They caused so much damage and destruction that there was a large increase in property insurance, especially in the area I purchased about a block from the water. I was fortunate there was no damage to my prospective new home.

Because I wanted to complete my new purchase, I had no choice but to come up with an additional $1,800 at closing for insurance alone. Out of the blue, the realtor who sold me this property called me and asked if I would like to have a renter for a short time. The prospective renter's property had been damaged during the storm, and he needed a temporary home. Would I! This would be great, as I hadn't planned to move from Atlanta for a year. I had lived in Atlanta for twenty-three years, and I needed to begin the arduous process of sorting and packing my things.

I asked my new renter for the first and last month rent check at the beginning of our agreement. Yes, the amount covered what I needed for insurance with four dollars left to spare. The renter stayed until my Atlanta house sold and the damages to his home were repaired completely—the exact time I was ready to move in. I couldn't have asked for better timing. God provided me revenue while I prepared for my new beginning. We were both blessed.

Note from Susan:

See Millie's story of how she found this property under "God's Property."

From Performance to the Real Thing
Mark Meena
Atlanta, Georgia

Performance, performance, performance, striving, goals, never enough and never good enough. I was always trying to please, to compete, and do better. This was my family environment growing up, and there was more of the same at church. I was always trying to strive to be good enough, and of course, I never was. I did not have a good picture of God. I felt He must hate me, and the feeling was mutual, I might add. What kind of a God was this? I never measured up anywhere. As I finished school and went on to college, nothing changed. I carried the same mindset right along with me.

I don't like to admit this, but I felt everything was about me, me, and me. If I did anything for anyone, it was for what benefit I may reap. Food, money, and sex—that describes what I was about. God didn't enter my mind much. He was at the bottom of the totem pole. My dating life involved giving lavish gifts—money was no problem, and I knew I could buy people. Money became my God.

My language would make anyone blush. Picture a spoiled, rotten, out-of-control teenager in an adult's body, someone intent on always having his way, and that was me.

I have a good business aptitude, and my gift involved troubleshooting for companies and turning them around or helping them become more successful. I was a financial success. Because I was very skilled at this, people put up with my putrid behavior. As you might suspect, I was not successful with long-term relationships. I thought other people were just difficult if they didn't go along with me. In my twenties, my family was not of much use to me either. After all, they did not benefit me much.

I must say I was quite the actor. I would put on a great show if I chose to by pretending to be generous, warm, and kind. I knew how to be a great host and could play the game. In business, I did not always do the right thing. Ironically, I went to prison for something I did not do. This got my attention—having a prison record is not something I aspired to.

Later on in my life, I realized what a wonderful thing this was because it got my attention in a serious way.

It began to dawn on me if I kept on the same track and continued to do some of the things I was doing, I could get into serious trouble.

I wasted no time telling people I was the greatest person in the world. I was in a serious love relationship and was crushed when my girlfriend ended it. How could she do this? I was such a great guy. Something must be wrong with her. After all, didn't I lavish her with gifts and take her to the best places? What more could she want?

Now I am older and wiser, at least a little bit, and I realize if you know you are all right, you don't have to spend time telling others how wonderful you are. But until I came to this realization, I felt I could fool others—perhaps myself most of all. My secretary at work gave me a little trophy with the word "greatest" on it. Smart woman, she knew how to keep her job!

I had plenty of money, no girlfriend or friends, and a family I was not thrilled about. Something was missing in my life. One day, someone told me about North Point Community Church in Atlanta, and I decided I would check it out. I found the church, not knowing what time the services were. The parking lot was crowded, so I decided to park and walk in. The service had started, and I was there in time to hear the minister giving the last of a series of talks on "The New Me." The minister Andy Stanley's words captured my interest. It was amazing I was in a church at all. Now I realize how fortunate I was to take the time to explore something outside of myself.

At Easter, I decided I would go to church again and ended up back to the same church. I have to say I felt very welcomed there, and the fact so many were attending made me think there must be some reason for their interest. Thousands of people sang in worship, and they seemed to enjoy it. I saw all ages, but especially lots of young people and young families. This piqued my interest.

I began attending the services each Sunday, and I surprised myself by enrolling in a course at the church about God and what a relationship with Him can be like. I liked the people in the class because they did not judge me, and they were interested in answering my questions. The most important thing I noticed was these people did not want anything from me except to be helpful and supportive. That was new for me—giving without expectations—and it made me want to know more. I started going to an area fellowship, a group of people that meet once a week to study the Bible or a series of teachings.

At one of the classes, one of the facilitators, David, was discussing the fruits of the Spirit. I had no idea what he was talking about, and this whetted my appetite even more. After he finished his talk, a question-and-answer session followed. I asked specifically how a person finds God. Again, my questions were answered with warmth and sincerity and with others sharing personal stories. There was no judgment in their attitude or answers. I told David I didn't understand much about the Bible, so David arranged to meet with me one-on-one at a later time. He continued to do this, and one day, he asked me if he could pray. I agreed. It was on May 5, 2002, that I made a decision to accept Jesus into my heart and repent of all my sins. This experience was a life change for me—the most important thing I have ever done. I saw God and people through different eyes. The empty places in my heart that I tried to fill with money and everything else are now being filled with God.

I remained in a small group and have learned to connect with others. I also led a Crown Ministries small group. This was a course on finances related to the spiritual and practical aspects of money, and I loved helping others in my business aptitude.

I was on the right path and thankful to the people who helped me on my journey. The second most important decision I made was to be baptized in July 2002. God was working with me just where I was and helping me along the path to follow Him. He wasn't waiting for me to become "good" before He walked alongside me.

One day, I was listening to a speaker from Campus Crusade for Christ. She was explaining to us that all we do is for the glory of God. The light bulb went off in my head. I understood what she said and asked if I could help in the ministry so I could share all I have learned with others.

I thought back to the first time I attended North Point Church and heard the minister speaking about "The New Me." And I began to realize there was a new me. I stopped cursing, and I started changing to other-centered from self-centered. My new prayer was "replace my heart with your heart, God." I wanted the will of God and His guidance in my life.

I began to pray for patience, and guess what happened? I had a flat tire while driving, pulled into a parking lot to change it, and couldn't remove the lug nut. Next, I had to call for a tow truck and a rental car, and this took up most of my day. Again, I was not upset. Before the new me, I would have been cursing and yelling at the tow truck driver and the rental car company and anybody else that happened to be around. I would have been furious about losing the entire day just because of a flat tire. You would not have wanted your children to see or hear me. The next day, I returned the rental car and went to Starbucks to read a book called *Brokenness* written by Nancy DeMoss. It is about pride and patience and the fact that God has a time frame in His plan. I knew I was finally getting this into my stubborn head.

God redirected my focus and changed some of my business. Although my income decreased, my needs are being met through Christ because I am Christ-centered. My focus is redirected to how I can impact lives. I have a good relationship with my family now. I have true friends I care about as much as they care about me. I pray for all of us every day and sincerely want to do God's will. The old me is gone. Good riddance, thank you very much. And I am sure my family, friends, and associates would agree with this!

Note from Susan:

I met Mark when he was one of the facilitators at a class I was taking at the church and remember him mentioning briefly God had changed his life. I had not met Mark until that class, and I wanted to find out what changed him from a self-centered person (as described by him) to a Christ-centered person. I asked him if he would be willing to share his story. I thought it fascinating and appreciate his candor and willingness to share with others. This is someone who really is filled with the fruits of the Holy Spirit—a man who at one time wasn't even aware of what they were. Now Mark is teaching about those very things. I learned quite a bit from the eight-week course he taught on this subject.

For those who are interested, here is a brief summary of the fruits of the spirit.

> But the fruit of the Spirit is love, joy, peace, longsuffering, kindness, goodness, faithfulness, gentleness and self-control. (Galatians 5:22)

A capsule version from the course Mark taught follows in a brief outline of the fruits of the spirit. The absence of these qualities produces many of the following symptoms:

Sleep/appetite disturbance, loss of energy and concentration, escape into work, drugs, infidelity, pornography, depressed mood, impatience and quick temper, controlling behaviors, obsessive-compulsive and loss of joy, love, affection, and romance.

Our wrong desires are	*The fruit of the Spirit is*
Evil	Good
Destructive	Productive
Easy to ignite	Difficult to ignite
Difficult to stifle	Easy to stifle
Self-centered	Self-giving

Oppressive and possessive	Liberating and nurturing
Decadent	Uplifting
Sinful	Holy
Deadly	Abundant life

What I took away from this information is doing things our way is not the best idea. Our way or God's—you decide.

God's Property
Millie Ross
Orange Beach, Alabama

I have lived in Atlanta for many years and made a decision to find a property out of state in Gulf Shores, Alabama. If I found something I liked, I would then get my longtime home ready to put on the market. I would start packing up many years of things and a lifetime of memories and change my life.

This move would be a major life-changing move for me, so I began to research different areas near the beach. I love the water and the sand, and the water imparts a sense of calmness to me. My brother and his family also live in Gulf Shores, so I knew I wanted to be in that area of the country. I prayed frequently for God to direct me to the property He thought would be best for me.

On my first scouting trip, I decided on one area in particular near the water and told the real estate agent to let me know if anything became available on two specific streets, either Wilson Street or Avenue D.

I returned home to Atlanta. I spoke with my real estate agent often, but nothing developed in the next six-month time period, so I gave up the idea of those two streets. I began looking in another area in Destin, Florida, several hours away. In this second area, I found a piece of land I liked and decided I would have my real estate agent write a contract the next day for this property. The day arrived, and right before I met with my real estate agent in Destin, I received a call from the realtor I had worked with in Gulf Shores. With excitement, she told me a house had become available on Avenue D, one of those two streets we had talked about months ago, and she thought I should take a look. I immediately called the second realtor and told her I might have found something else.

I drove to Gulf Shores to see the house, and I liked it right away. The location was perfect, and my next step was to decide what to offer. After ignoring advice from several people who suggested higher prices, I made an offer at a lower price. With only one counteroffer, I was able to purchase the property for close to my original price—several thousand dollars less than everyone suggested.

I was very pleased with my new purchase. The land I almost purchased was in a much higher price range; the house I bought in Gulf Shores was much more comfortable for me financially.

I knew if I were supposed to have this property in Gulf Shores, it would work out. And that is just what happened. You see, since the beginning of the time when I decided to make the decision to move, I had been asking God to direct me to the right location at a price that was right for me. And He did just in time!

Note from Susan

I could only picture Millie's new home from her description, and when I visited her, I could see why she fell in love with it. The location is wonderful, and with a few improvements, she has truly made it "Home Sweet Home."

Hi, Mom and Dad
Julie Barnes
Duluth, Georgia

Being a mom is something I desired with all my heart, and my husband and I tried for several years to have a child. Every time I saw someone who was pregnant or had a child, I wanted to change places. I looked at moms and dads with their little ones, and my heart longed to have a child of our very own. When a baby shower invitation arrived in the mail, I was happy for others and looked forward to the day there would be a baby shower for my little one. However, as the months went by, the desire and disappointment got harder and harder to bear. We overextended ourselves financially with doctor visits and tests in a search for a solution to this challenge. And we never got the news we waited so desperately to hear.

One day, we came to the realization that although we may not be able to conceive our own child, we still wanted to be parents. We began to consider adoption, something we would not have thought of several years before. We gathered information and began the process, and one wonderful day, we got the phone call we prayed for. We became the parents of a beautiful and smart baby girl. She is now over two years old, and we are ecstatic to have her in our life. Jenna Grace, our little angel, is named after my best friend who lost her life to breast cancer five days after Jenna was born. Her namesake lives on in this vivacious creature God has "graced" us with.

What I would like to share with others is that my husband and I had no doubt this little one was to be raised by us. God has the ultimate plan even though we can't always see it clearly at the time from our vantage point.

Note from Susan:

It was fun hearing about Jenna. She is very precocious, and everyone delights in her company. I would say she is the light of her parents' lives.

Home Sweet Home
Margaret Lee
Tampa, Florida

In 2003, the interest rates were still low, and I was tired of renting. All I could think about was buying my very own home. One day, as I was looking at houses advertised on the Internet, I found a home in a neighborhood I was familiar with. I wasted no time as I took down the address. Jumping into my car a few minutes later, I drove to the neighborhood. When I pulled up, I thought to myself, *this is it*. I knocked on the door, and the owner opened it. She told me she was a realtor and had just put it on the Internet; it was love at first sight, not for the realtor but for the house. I found my dream—it was just what I wanted. I knew this was the house I was going to buy.

I applied for a loan, and my credit was horrid. Although I was not surprised, I didn't give up. I talked to bankers and mortgage brokers; they pulled my credit report and told me I was too high a risk. I finally found a mortgage broker who worked diligently and found a lender who would work with me. The interest rate would be a little higher as the risk was higher. The first credit report showed some problems. I was told the mortgage broker needed to check it again one more time, and the lender would make a decision at that time. For some unexplainable reason, my credit showed no problems the next time the report was pulled. The issues seemed to have been taken care of, and the loan was approved.

Before closing, the lender checked the credit one last time, and the original problems showed again. This is the amazing part to me—the lender approved the loan based on the previous report. They could have canceled the loan. Something made them decide to take the risk.

This entire lending process took a long time, and many times, the situation for finding a lender and closing on the house did not look good. Against many odds, I felt a peace about the situation most of the time. There were a few times I would panic, and then I reminded myself God was in charge, and if I was to have a house, I would. I had been praying for the right house to buy before I found the house and was sure things would work out in the end, and they did. I am a happy homeowner. This is a great home for me, and I know I am where I am supposed to be at this time in my life. God has blessed me.

MORE THAN A COINCIDENCE

The Loaves and the Fishes
Millie Ross
Orange Beach, Alabama

Whenever I need a little faith, I think about my uncle who died in Selma, Alabama, quite a few years ago. Although I lived in Atlanta at the time, I told my cousins I would prepare all the food for their dad's get-together at the church after the funeral service. They lived far away, and I knew it would be difficult for them. Mom lived in Selma, so I could prepare all the food at her house. I shopped, and everything was ready to be set out at my mother's house after the service. It was up to my mother and me. The thing was, I had no idea how many people would attend the service until that day. As the service began and I looked around, I knew I was in trouble. *There are more than fifty people here. I can't believe this many came to the service. Okay, Lord, You are going to have to help with this—like the loaves and fishes stories in the Bible.*

As I left the service, I thought about the ham I had bought, two 9 x 13 pans of green beans, two pineapple casseroles, bread, a few cakes, drinks, and a few other items that were at my mom's house. *This is not enough for this crowd.* I wanted to stop to pick up an emergency portion of food but decided against it because I didn't have time to get anything before people started arriving at my mom's house. I will just have to make the best with what I have. Do you think anyone brought any extra food? Nope, except for one person who brought a cake. "We better wait to eat until everyone has prepared their plate," I suggested to my mother. It is rather embarrassing to run out of food.

I still can't believe it to this day when I think about what happened. To my surprise, we had enough food for everyone; some people went back for seconds, and there were still leftovers. Some people reading this may think this was an exaggeration, but it is not. I wouldn't believe it myself if I wasn't there in the middle of it. Just another example of God behind the scenes—He is present even in the smallest of details. But then most of us have heard the story about the loaves and fishes in the Bible where Jesus fed the multitudes.

Note from Susan

Mathew 14:15–21, Mark 6:35–44, and John 6:5–14 all refer to the five thousand people who were fed by Jesus with only five loaves of bread and two fishes.

Mathew 15:32–38 and Mark 8:1–9 refer to the miracle of four thousand people fed with seven loaves of bread and a few fishes. Miracles happened during Jesus's time, and they happen around us if we ask for the eyes to see them.

Millie and I are great friends, and she does not exaggerate. She tells it like it is—her word is gold.

Mom, We're on the Way
Helen Kenny
Roswell, Georgia

My husband and I were thrilled to be expecting triplets, three for the price of one. I had problems since the beginning of the pregnancy, and on February 13, 2001, a day I will never forget, I found myself in labor and succumbed to fear. It is difficult to put into words our feelings about the possibility I could lose our babies, a thought I tried to put out of my mind. The truth is my husband and I both knew the possibility of our babies surviving at this early stage of pregnancy was highly unlikely.

We rushed to the hospital, and they hurried me into the emergency room. My doctor gave me an epidural. This procedure didn't work, and we found out later this was fortunate. My doctor then gave me general anesthesia, and he, along with his team, were able to stop labor and reverse the process. Baby Katherine, who was trying to be born, was pushed back into the uterus. With sutures, my doctor was able to keep the babies in place—this in itself was an amazing medical procedure to me. If the epidural had taken place, he would not have been able to perform this procedure.

We thought everything was fine and calmed down. A short time later, I went into labor again. A nurse on duty (an angel) recognized my distended bladder was interrupting the pregnancy. When the doctor corrected this problem, my labor ceased. If this medical team had not diagnosed the problem, all of my triplets would not be here today. God had the right team in place for my little ones at just the right time at the right hospital. We now have our hands full, and we are thankful every day for our three little ones. God is in control.

Note from Susan:

This story is especially poignant as I begin writing this on Mother's Day 2005. Thank you for sharing this very personal story to give encouragement to others. I have three sons, and they are almost four years apart. Just taking care of them, if they had been triplets, would have been overwhelming for me. Happy Mother's Day to all who are blessed to have children.

No Butts about It
Anonymous
Atlanta, Georgia

About thirty-five years ago, my husband smoked about two to three packs of cigarettes a day. He made the Marlboro Man proud! My husband wanted to stop, but every time he tried, he became irritable—yep, grouchy! Anyone who has been around someone trying to stop this habit can identify. It is not pleasant for any of us.

One day, my husband who had just become a Christian, was walking and walking around our yard. He was talking to the Lord, saying, "Lord, if you are real, please take this terrible habit from me." From that very day to this, his desire to smoke evaporated into thin air. That was the end of it—God got my husband's attention and showed His presence in a real way. And I am so thankful to have such a wonderful Christian man to call my husband and so thankful that God answered my husband's plea for help.

Pain-Free
Ann Dozetos
Fort Pierce, Florida

Clutching my chest, I thought to myself, *I must be dying.* At home in bed, in the dark of night, the searing pain caught me unprepared. I scuffled to the bathroom and rummaged through the medicine cabinet. I found various medications and tried one that seemed to help. I finally closed my eyes and nodded off to sleep. In the morning, I felt fine. *Good*, I thought, *I don't want anything to interrupt my travel plans.* In two days, I was flying to Houston to visit my sister. The pain had been unbearable last night, but I thought I was fine now.

I continued with my plans to meet my husband and several friends for lunch the same day. As we sat in the restaurant, I was again struck with the same crippling pain in the same location. Clutching my chest, I eked out a few barely audible words. My husband took me to the doctor where I underwent tests. No reason for my pain surfaced. My doctor prescribed medication, and I began to take it to keep the pain at bay. I decided to continue with my travel arrangements and flew to Houston the next day. I didn't feel great, but I could function.

Still in some pain and on medication, I accompanied my sister to the bazaar at her church. While we were walking around, the parish priest came by. My sister asked him if he would pray for me to be healed of the cause of my pain. She told him about the seriousness of the pain, and he wasted no time praying for me. After he finished the prayers, the pain disappeared. I discontinued the pain medication, and the pain has never returned. This was one and a half years ago, and I know that this was not an accident. I consider this a miracle because of the intensity of the pain and know the Greatest Healer of all healed me. He answered our prayer.

MORE THAN A COINCIDENCE

Priceless beyond Measure
Susan E. Hall
Atlanta, Georgia

One of my friends from Florida visited me in Atlanta in the summer of 2003. We had a full day planned. First, I needed to dash across the street to the neighborhood drugstore to buy a birthday card. I left my Florida friend at my house, and in a hurry, I ran across the parking lot, found a card, paid for it, and was almost at the exit door. At that point, a woman came up to me and asked if my name was Susan. I answered with a surprised "yes." Something seemed familiar, but everything was out of my context.

My heart did a little flutter when she introduced herself as Peggy. Peggy and I had been best friends in high school many, many years ago (I'm not fessing up how long ago). We lost contact after high school, marriages, divorce (yep, I hate that part, but it is true), and life's many twists and turns. Our mothers had also been best friends. We now have grown children of our own, and both of our parents are deceased. I was thrilled we "bumped" into each other.

This turned out to be a day that neither of us will ever forget and a subsequent answer to a prayer of mine. The company I was with in 2000 moved me to Atlanta from my long-time Florida home. After three years of constant traveling in the southeast, I had just taken a new position that did not require travel. My previous schedule allowed me little time to connect with people in my new location, but now I prayed I would meet some great Christian women who would become friends.

Peggy said she had seen me scurrying across the drugstore parking lot that sunny summer day and, although she didn't see my face, she thought it might be me. Now the fact Peggy recognized me from the back makes me laugh—well, we will not go there. Maybe this is a fact I should have omitted from this story. Who wants to be recognized from the back!

Peggy and I reconnected—as if we had seen each other only days ago. Peggy told me she seldom stopped at that shopping center. Combined with my impulse to pick up a birthday card in the same center she thought the timing perfect. We both agree this was not a coincidence—it was divine, not a coincidence. Through Peggy, I met other wonderful women and some of us became friends as well.

We both love telling this story. I have been blessed beyond measure with priceless friends. As a matter of fact, we could hardly wait to get this story in this book. Sometimes God answers even the smallest of prayers in fascinating ways. Lucky me!

Time for a New Model—Not!
Anonymous
Atlanta, Georgia

I want to keep going right past my house, yep, I want to keep on driving somewhere else. My thoughts astounded me.

The thought of running away from my life sounded like a great idea even though the guilt tore at my heart. After a long day of work, my family expected me to come home like I always did. On the other hand, two of my good friends had done exactly what I was thinking—left their wives with broken hearts, and the pieces of their children's lives scattered in the dust. *But who cares*, I thought, *you only live once! My family will just have to adjust.* Then I grimaced, knowing deep down this wasn't the case.

I felt conflicted and stuck, angry and bitter. I love my family deeply and know the importance of family values, yet I felt trapped in my emotions. I had trouble concentrating, was overwhelmed with confusion, and felt there was more to life. I cried out to God to help me. As if He needed my help, I had two solutions for Him: Just take me to heaven or show me how to get out of my feelings of desolation, hurt, and bitterness. I felt like I was stuck in the bottom of a pit.

There is a critical and "typical" period in many men's lives known as the midlife crisis. This excruciating time propels some of us to do more than get a red sports car, run triathlons, and change our wardrobe. We want to flee our mundane home life of "is this all there is?" and "is it possible we may not be young forever?" Even better, someone else besides our wives can erase our thoughts and insecurities. A little adventure will help us find what we may be missing. Of course, it wouldn't be so bad if that "someone else" were a little younger either—maybe a little thinner and more enticing. The interesting woman will make us look more interesting as well and reflect on us that we still have "it."

Well, God in His wisdom didn't give me the "easy" way out by sending me to heaven. Nope. He sent real people to help me change myself. It is difficult to change when it would seem that instead God should change everything and everyone else around us. Men know how to fix things; that's what we do best. There must be a quick answer to fix this craziness.

God sent me an answer via US mail—an invitation to a marriage conference to be held in Memphis, Tennessee, by Intimate Life Ministries (Dr. David and Teresa Ferguson) based in Austin, Texas. This invitation included a complimentary seminar, plus three nights and four days at the Peabody, a beautiful hotel near the riverfront in downtown Memphis. In addition, all the conference materials and meals were complimentary. I paid absolutely no attention. I knew there was a huge catch—you just don't get something for nothing. Naturally, I threw this lifeline in the trash. Who would send all this for free?

Well, so glad you asked! God wasn't through with me yet. One day, several weeks later, one of my friends from church asked me if I received the invitation to a marriage conference to be held in Memphis! My friend knew I was considering going into the ministry, and he thought this conference would be helpful to me. Little did this man know how much I needed to go and not for the reasons he thought!

I rethought the invitation and decided that my wife and I would attend. We drove the eight hours from Atlanta. Although we both were used to avoiding conflict, we found ourselves arguing and fussing all the way. We either needed a marriage conference or a boxing ring and gloves! I was tempted to turn the car around and head back home, but something kept me plodding on. I do hate to give up.

I had no clue my earlier cry for help was about to be answered but not in the way I ever imagined. God likes to surprise us! The next four days turned out to be some of the most life-changing hours for me. The Holy Spirit entered my soul. Ugly poisons and hurts came to light and left me healed. I loved my wife but didn't know how to show her my love or accept hers. Those four days of introspection and prayer gave me the knowledge I needed.

I now understand why people give up on their marriages—they think the love they are looking for is gone. My wife and I received the truth that set both of us free to love each other again. "It was a wonderful journey of discovery and healing. I learned how to speak the truth in love, how to replace bad relationship skills with good ones, and how to forgive from the heart."

Jesus said in Mathew 18:35, "This is how my heavenly Father will treat each of us unless you forgive your brother from your heart." This is the parable of the unforgiving debtor. Consider reading Mathew chapter 18 for the background of this verse.

We will be shown the way if we ask and *truly* seek the truth. In my counseling work, I come across people with similar temptations. Experiencing this temptation has helped me in understanding others. What might look like the easy way out is not always easy. Repercussions can be horrendous in hindsight. The leaving spouse who is unwilling to find wise counsel just takes himself and all his problems with him into the next relationship.

I cried out to God for answers when I didn't even know the question. And the Wisest Teacher of all changed me.

Free At Last!
Keith Smoyer
Asheville, North Carolina

I am now twenty-three years old, and when I think about my twentieth year, I remember it was something else, and I don't mean in a good way. My mom, a single parent, was doing her best to raise me, and she was at her wit's end. I was into all kinds of destructive things. One night, I got into a fight that was pretty bad and ended up in the hospital facing surgery to repair the damage done to my face. The pills prescribed for pain helped fuel my desire for drugs, and it wasn't long before I was dealing in the drug Ecstasy.

MORE THAN A COINCIDENCE

I worked during the day as a roofer and found I was drawn to the party life, a venue that enabled me to sell drugs. One night, I was doing just that in Charlotte when they booted me out of the nightclub, taking my five hundred dollars—all the money I had on me. This money was given to me by one of my buddies, so now I needed to find a way to make some additional money quickly so I could repay him.

I felt pretty desperate. I figured I had been high on drugs for about eighteen hours when I decided to make a drug deal to bring in some money. One of the girls I met at the club went with me to Ashville to buy Ecstasy, and we then drove to a small town in South Carolina. It was there we met up with a man who agreed to buy $1,500 worth of drugs. The thought entered my mind that this man might be an undercover agent. Throwing caution to the wind—an easy thing to do when you are high on drugs—I went ahead with the transaction anyway. To my horror, we were immediately surrounded with the flashing lights of twenty-something police cars. Even in my condition, I knew this was not a good thing for me—I was busted! I told the police the girl with me was innocent—I did not want her to go to jail. This was something I got to do.

You might imagine how thrilled my mom and dad were to get that call from me, saying I was in jail. Not a proud moment for them. I must add something here. I felt relief in jail because now I could stop running. The charge was serious—six felonies and a seventy-five-thousand-dollar bond. I was appointed an attorney by the court.

Now in jail with no drugs or alcohol to keep me company and dull my senses, things could not have been much worse for me. I thought I had ruined my short life and felt hopeless. I had been raised in a Christian home, and I decided to cry out to the Lord God to help me. I was at the bottom.

One day in came a fifty-one-year-old man. My roommate, or I guess I should say cellmate, strung out on heroin, told me he had been in and out of jail for years. He also said when I got out of jail, I would be back again for sure. I did not ever want to be in jail again, and if I got a chance for probation, I sure didn't want to end up like this man.

My bail was reduced to ten thousand dollars, and both my parents bailed me out after twenty-nine days. This was a May I won't ever forget. The first week I got out of jail, I moved in with my father and was able to get my old roofing job back.

One rainy day, working was out of the question, and I weakened and went out with my old drinking buddies. I drank and drank and blacked out from four in the afternoon until two the next morning. The only good thing about this is the fact I was not in the car with my buddy who was arrested on a DUI charge. However, when I came to, I was a mess, didn't remember a thing, and didn't know where I was. I decided again I had to get in charge of my life.

Well, I lost my job again, and every night, detoxing and miserable, I was tempted to go out with my friends. I knew they were not a good influence on me, so I would go into my room, closed the door, hit the pillow, and cry. I was miserable and lonely.

It was during this time I began going to church with my dad and began to meet some people my age. One of the girls I met told me a visiting minister was coming to the church, and this man had performed miracles on some people. I knew I needed a healing and thought maybe I should check this minister out when he came to town. What could I lose! So I drove to the church that night and found myself sitting in the parking lot of the church, wondering if I should go in. All I kept seeing were old people going into the church. Then the girl I had been talking to pulled up into the church parking lot. I gathered up my courage, and I decided I would go in, and I sat behind her and her family.

I have to admit the minister gave an "awesome" talk, and for the first time ever, I took notes. Heck, in school I never took notes. Probably should have though. At the end of the service, the minister asked anyone who wanted prayer to come down front in the church. I decided I might as well. In front of me, I could see people falling to the floor after the minister laid his hands on them. I was not sure this was real and then thought to myself, *So what? It does not matter what anyone else thinks. This is between God and me anyway. So Your will be done.* I was serious—after the messes I made on my own steam, I knew I needed help.

Although a little nervous when the minister got closer and shook my hand, I heard him say something about giving all my prayers and concerns to the Lord. Then he let go of my hand. No one was touching me, yet something came upon me because I felt a tremendous pressure and fell backward. I was overcome with the presence of God, and I felt numb and tingly at the same time. I could not get up for what I was told was about ten minutes. I cried and realized for the first time God is real, good, and loving. I remember thinking I had tried alcohol, drugs, sex, and whatever I wanted to feel "cool," and it didn't work. I now know firsthand God is so much bigger than I can imagine. He is the only one who can fill the empty place in my soul. From that moment on, all my desire for drugs and alcohol, substances that had consumed my life, disappeared and never returned. It was the most moving experience of my young life.

After the service, I was about to leave the parking lot of the church when I had a strong desire to go back and speak to the minister. I did just this and told the minister I was different; I experienced the Holy Spirit for the first time. It is an experience I still have a hard time describing. I also began to get interested in Bible study and did begin to change my life. It wasn't always easy, and I had temptations, and I began to depend on the Lord to get me through. I could not do this in my own strength.

The day came for my court appearance, and due to the fact I had been attending church and Bible study during the interim, I was given a lesser sentence. The ten-year sentence I could have received was reduced to three years based upon my good behavior. Another change I made was ending a dating relationship I realized was not good for me, and I changed my friends as well. I knew I put my parents through grief and soon reunited with both of them. Both my parents and grandparents had been praying for me continually, and their prayers were finally answered.

God can do anything if you let Him into your life even when everything seems hopeless. To be ensnared with addictions of any kind that have such a stronghold on your life, and to know there is hope, and to be released from them immediately is a blessing that doesn't happen to everyone. I can say with certainty that being arrested was one of the best things that could have happened to me during that dark night of my soul!

CHAPTER 4

Wisdom

If any of you lacks wisdom, let him ask of God, who gives to all liberally and without reproach, and it will be given to him.
—James 1:5

SUSAN FISKUM HALL

My Hard-Earned Lesson of the Heart
Fran Stewart
Lawrenceville, Georgia

In 1972, I was living in Vermont, a young married woman in my twenties with no children. One of my friends was an irrepressibly funny woman in her midthirties. Ann was a talented poet.

She had two little girls, probably about six and eight years old at the time. Her husband was working out of state, and Ann had no transportation and little money. I had no idea how difficult this must have been for her while trying to raise two little girls with no physical, financial, or emotional help. I was clueless. Years later, when I had my own children to raise, I had an awakening. It had never dawned on me to offer my friend and neighbor a ride to the grocery store or surprise her with little gifts. I thought I was a good friend to her. I remember once Ann mentioned she had walked to the grocery store—a five-mile trip. I blithely replied, "Oh, what a lovely day it's been for a walk!" I never thought of offering her a ride to the grocery store or the Laundromat, which was also five miles away.

Both her little girls got chicken pox at the same time; and Ann, who never had the disease as a young child, became sick as well. I am sure she was worn out from taking care of two feverish and irritable little girls covered with red spots. I never thought about any of this at the time. I wasn't sure I had gotten this disease as a child myself, so I didn't offer to help. I didn't want to catch anything. I didn't take her meals. I did nothing—nothing.

One night at about ten o'clock, Ann called me, and I could hardly recognize her weak voice. Her breathing was labored, and in few barely audible words, she asked me if I could take her to the emergency room. This was the only time she ever asked for my help. I jumped in my car, drove to her trailer, and we took off. One of her neighbors had come over to watch her little girls. The trip was long, and I felt frantic. Ann could not lie down and was gasping for breath the entire way. Her appearance frightened me as well—angry spots covered her swollen face and every piece of exposed skin.

MORE THAN A COINCIDENCE

I remember my feeling of relief when we were greeted by a compassionate nurse at the hospital who put her arm around Ann's shoulder and said, "It looks like you don't feel so great," an understatement to say the least. She tenderly ushered Ann into the emergency room. I was surprised when Ann was admitted to intensive care. I knew she was sick but didn't realize just how serious the situation had become. I was told I didn't need to stay. Because I was not family, I was not allowed in her room. I felt helpless and would have done whatever I could to help but had no idea what that would be.

All this happened on a midweek night. I went home late that night. I did not know how to contact Ann's husband but found someone at the trailer park who was able to contact her husband the next day. I was not allowed to visit, so I called the hospital each day and was relieved when I was told Ann was doing better. On Sunday morning when I called, I was told that Ann had died during the night. I was stunned. I had expected Ann to recover. It was at that moment I realized I had been no help to her at all. Now it was too late to think of ways I could have been a better friend. Telling this story many years later still brings sadness to my heart.

Several nights later, I was still grieving for my friend. My husband stayed in the house while I took our two dogs out for their nightly walk. It was a perfectly clear evening. The stars and moon made the night look magical. The beauty of that starry night did little for my mood. I was feeling sadness and remorse for what happened. How I wished I had made Ann's life a little easier when I had the chance. I remember kicking myself mentally.

It was about 10:30 p.m. as I walked up the path to where the dogs were running and romping. I felt a distinct presence on my right as if someone was beside me. As I turned my head in that direction, I saw a little cloud—that's the only way I know how to describe it. It was about the size of someone's head and level with mine. I could not believe what I was seeing, and I am sure my eyes widened with surprise. When I turned, the cloud turned; when I went ahead, it was there beside me. I stopped, and it stopped. I felt calm and had no trace of fear or danger as if this occurrence was nothing out of the ordinary. I had an awareness, a certainty that it was Ann. I have never had such an experience of knowing like this. I broke into tears. As they streamed down my face, I told her I was so sorry. I don't know if I heard her answer or simply felt it, but I will never forget her words. "I'm perfectly fine now," she said. "You did the best you could. And...I...chose...to...go." The sentences were deliberate, and she stressed each word. Still crying, I told her I missed her so much, and before I could say anything else, the cloud disappeared. I felt calmness and peace flow over me and felt Ann was in a better place. It was at that moment I realized how difficult her life had been. Much later, I heard her girls went to live with their grandmother.

That is not the end of the story. Five years later, I began a new job in the office of a family dentist. I was talking with a woman as she paid her bill, and I noticed she worked at the hospital in the intensive care unit where Ann died. I found myself thanking her. "I had a good friend who was in intensive care some time ago," I told her. "Even though she died, I know she got the best of care while she was there."

The nurse replied that she enjoyed her job and liked to help people. "But," she said, "there was one patient I always wondered about." She continued on to say the patient had been improving, but then without warning, she died. The nurse said, "I always wondered what we did wrong."

"Was her name Ann?" I asked and mentioned Ann's last name.

With a look of shock on her face and surprise in her eyes, she told me this was the patient she was referring to. I told her about my experience after Ann's death, and when I said that Ann had told me she had chosen to leave, she thanked me for sharing my story. As a matter of fact, she came behind my desk and hugged me, saying that I had finally brought her peace about that whole experience.

I know God brought all the pieces together that day in the dental office. I had the opportunity to meet the nurse who helped care for Ann, and I was able to let her know she had done all she could as well. I was in just the right place in the dental office when the nurse who just "happened" to be a patient of the dentist came in for the first time in more than a year.

Although Ann was not in my life for a long period, she changed my life by her presence. She broadened my awareness of insight and compassion and gave me the gift of her forgiveness. I believe God brought the nurse and me together so we could find peace about this woman who passed through our lives.

Note from Susan

When Fran told me this story, I thought how amazing life can be and how we can be changed forever in an instant. I heard the catch in her voice when she first told me about Ann's death. It is many years later, but the experience is still alive in her heart.

Another thing I think interesting is Fran's mention of Ann's talent of writing poetry. Fran began on the writing path many years later, and she is now a published author. She writes gentle murder mysteries and has the distinguished honor of being a Georgia Author of the Year Award winner. She writes for the sheer joy of it. If you would like to read more about her, I encourage you to please check out her website at www.franstewart.com. You can read more about Fran and her work.

I am thankful I have had the opportunity to meet her through the Georgia Writers Association. When I told her what I was writing about, she offered to share several of her experiences for others to see how the flow of Spirit moves through our lives in so many different ways. Please read about her other life-changing experience in this book in the story called "More Than a Tractor Trailer."

Moments in Time
GiGi Hackford
Fairhope, Alabama

Recently, I was sitting at my computer, and his name came into my mind. I hadn't thought about Rufus in years.

About fifteen years ago, in my early forties, I met a gentleman who became a great friend. I was teaching at the time in New York, and he was from Boston. He was fluent in German and French, and we had many interesting philosophical discussions. He had many friends who enjoyed conversations with him as well. Not afraid to be who he was, he was brilliant yet humble. I would add he was a generous man with a European flair. After a time, I moved to the south, and somehow we lost touch.

I decided I would see if I could find him and did an internet search. I found a website that was talking about him and reviewing some of his published work. It wasn't until I got to the end of the website that I found out he had died several years ago. My heart just dropped when I realized I would never be able to talk with him again.

This moment was an epiphany for me. Time easily slips away. I made up my mind. I would spend mine very carefully and never again fritter my time away on mindless pursuits. Something happened in my spirit, and I decided to take my artwork more seriously than I have ever done before. I teach children and love every moment of it and paint for a living, but my painting is what feeds my spirit and gives me joy. Although a difficult decision because I don't have an endless supply of time, next year, I will paint full-time.

Time is such a gift—spend it wisely and do what you are meant to do. I am doing that now like never before. Thank you for showing me, my old and dear friend.

Note from Susan

I met GiGi at the Fairhope Art Gallery in Fairhope, Alabama. Her artwork caught my attention. The piece she was working on was vibrant, and it made me feel alive just looking at it.

CHAPTER 5

Comfort

Trust in the Lord with all your heart, And lean not on your own understanding. In all your ways acknowledge Him, And He shall direct your paths
—Proverbs 3:5–6

A Penny for Your Thoughts
Judy Zimmerman
Snellville, Georgia

Did you ever have a time in your life when you just didn't know how you were going to make it? Perhaps if I share a little of my story, you may find some comfort when there doesn't seem to be any.

My husband, Carl, was struggling with cancer, and we had to face the fact that sometimes we don't get the healing we pray for and want. Our journey began when we received the devastating doctor's report. We had been married for years and had expectations we would be having many more anniversaries together. This news was a defining moment in our lives. I remember we were in the doctor's office and how we heard the words but didn't seem to comprehend them. The doctor's mouth was moving, and I felt a strange numbness and detachment as if his words were for someone else. I felt weak and could feel the sensation of the blood draining from my face. Our world seemed to stop that day.

Not too long after, Carl checked into the hospital at Northside in Atlanta. When I went to visit, I always took the front elevators. I don't know why I decided to take the back elevator that day, but I did. Alone in the elevator, I spied a shiny penny on the floor. Out of character for me, I decided to pick it up and put it into my wallet. A few days later, I was talking to my sister, and for some unknown reason, I told her about the penny. After a moment of silence, my sister asked me what was written on the penny. I didn't know what she meant. "In God We Trust," she responded. I thought about this and again, not knowing why, I opened my wallet to see if the penny was there. My heart jumped a little when I saw it tucked in a side compartment. I moved it to a place in my wallet for safekeeping so I wouldn't spend it.

I visited my husband every day. The weeks passed slowly, and I felt a mix of emotions from day to day and sometimes moment to moment. One day I felt hopeful, other times I felt hopeless, angry, and sad. How could this be happening? There were many times of exhaustion, and fear would fill my soul. I tried to be strong for

Carl and our son, and many times, I just couldn't hold everything together. One day, when I was getting ready to go the hospital, I was so upset I dissolved into tears and could hardly see to drive as tears streamed down my face. I didn't know how I could get through watching my husband suffer day by day with no hope of recovery. I was going through the motions of trying to make everything seem ordinary for our son and the rest of the family. As I went to my car parked in the driveway, I happened to look down and saw a dull penny. I remembered "In God We Trust," and I calmed down and headed to the hospital.

Carl continued getting weaker and weaker. His illness took its toll on me and the rest of the family as well. One day, I sent the doctor an email with questions regarding my husband and was very upset when I didn't have a response from him. The questions I had asked were tough ones. I felt at rock bottom. When I thought about my life before with my healthy husband and our son and our nice life together, I could not imagine what was going to happen if Carl was no longer with us. Alone in these thoughts, I was walking up the sidewalk to the hospital to visit my husband when on the sidewalk in front of me was a dull penny. Of course, I picked it up. I went into the hospital room and not long after this, the doctor entered the room and apologized for not responding to my email. He spent some time talking with me, and it was one of the best conversations we ever had.

I felt like a zombie during this time, and it was helpful to have the concern of friends. Even a simple email, phone call, or a neighbor's homemade meal showed me how people do care. One couple from our church would call me every Saturday for an update on my husband's condition. I decided it was time to share my story about the pennies I kept finding and told them what kept happening. They asked if they could tell the Sunday school class my story. I agreed. My heart was touched by their concern.

One day, not too long after this conversation, I received a card from the Sunday school class. They had used the computer to design an angel on the front of the card and scripted inside was a penny prayer for my husband, our son Jason, and me with our names.

Inside, they glued a shiny penny with the words "In God We Trust" at the top. Underneath were the words to a prayer. This act of kindness lifted our spirits in ways you cannot even imagine. We were warmed with their concern that we were in their prayers on a constant basis. They also told me that the class had begun to send these angel penny cards to ailing members of their church.

A month or so after this, my husband almost died. I kept thinking as I kept watch by his bedside in intensive care that I really needed a penny of encouragement. I thought about all the times I would get upset, and it was at that point I would find a penny. A sense of calmness would wash over me when I remembered that God was in charge, and I needed to trust Him. As day crept into nightfall, my brother and I, exhausted from sitting by my husband's bedside for hours, decided to go to the hospital snack bar. It was late, and we were the only ones there. We placed our order, and then I saw it—a dull penny on the counter.

The days dragged on, and my husband got worse—he was so sick he was moved to a hospice center. We knew the end was near. His fever was very high. He was unable to speak. We heard that hearing is the last sense to go, so the entire family surrounded his bedside and told Carl it was all right for the angels to take him to heaven.

At that point, my sister-in-law searched through the drawers in the hospital room for more washcloths to put on my husband's forehead to cool him off. I needed a break and stepped outside the room for a moment to try to prepare myself. When I returned to the room, she showed me the only thing she had found—the shiny penny in the third drawer. Every other drawer was empty.

I told my husband what his sister found. Fifteen minutes later, with all of his family members surrounding him with their love, Carl took his final breath. It was then I remembered the shiny penny I found at the very beginning of this journey. All the other pennies I had found were dull except for this shiny penny at the end!

At the memorial service, the family gathered a collage of photos of Carl's life. One picture showed him wearing his uniform in a bunker in Vietnam. It was then we saw the words on his helmet. We had seen the photo before but hadn't noticed the helmet. Carl never spoke about the war. We could barely read the words he had printed across his helmet: "In God I Trust."

Note from Susan

The first time I was privileged to hear this story was when I attended Carl's funeral with a friend. I had not yet met his wife Judy. After the service, my friend told me that Judy had never spoken in front of a large group. I was truly amazed. She looked very comfortable as she told this story, and due to the occasion, I wondered how anyone could speak at a memorial service with such composure. Her story brought tears to my eyes and many others then and now as I write this story.

It was sometime later I decided to begin to write this book. Because I thought what Judy shared was truly beautiful and inspiring, I asked her if I could use this story of how she was reminded to trust even in the saddest of circumstances even though she didn't understand.

Interestingly enough, this story has been an inspiration to me in the writing of this book. The fact that I would even consider writing a book is amazing to me.

And I, who used to always step over pennies, shiny or not, have been surprised at how many pennies I keep finding. They never cease to remind me that God is truly trustworthy. And the pennies I find, for the most part, are shiny.

During a job transition on a really trying day, I got out of my car at a fast-food restaurant, and there they were—eight shiny pennies in a perfect circle right beside my car on the pavement and, yes, not a dull one in the bunch. Guess I needed extra encouragement that day!

I have had to put this book on hold for about almost two years due to a new demanding job I had and wondered when I could get back to writing. Just a few weeks ago, as I left church, I looked down at the chairs as I left the row, and on the seat was a shiny penny—rather unusual when you consider just a few minutes ago someone had most probably been sitting there. Last week, I happened to glance under the desk I was using at work, and in a container, right on top, sat a shiny penny.

However, the one incident that I found most incredible of all happened on a dreary, rainy Atlanta Sunday in 2007. I was in a long line of traffic just waiting to leave the church parking lot and was almost at the intersection manned by several policemen directing traffic. My windows were up, and they were tinted at that. One of the policemen came over to my car, and as I unrolled the window, he handed me a penny, saying that this was for me. He had to walk several car lengths, and I was so surprised all I remember is saying thank you. I take all these as signs to just continue to trust no matter what is happening. I have had countless shiny pennies in my path, and I am always being reminded to trust that Jesus is just working behind the scenes.

Those are just a few examples I am sharing with you, and today I am returning to my labor of love and am continuing to complete the book.

A Sign of Life
Kathy Gidus
Casselberry, Florida

I can't believe it—I wasn't at my dad's side. He had been sick for several weeks, and we all knew he was not to get any better. The hospital visits were many and sad as our family kept vigil by his bedside. I made many visits during this difficult time of the inevitable.

I had just come home from visiting my dad in the hospital, and I decided I needed to be outside. Gardening is my way of relieving stress. I love working with my plants and flowers. I began weeding and trying to quiet my mind. I knew my dad would not be alive much longer, and my sad thoughts persisted.

I was weeding the orchid tree I had planted in my yard about four or five years before. It had grown into a healthy tree but never bloomed. I waited each year with expectation. Today it looked the same as usual. I reflected that the orchid was my father's favorite flower. I continued to weed around the tree when I noticed a bloom near the bottom of the tree, the first bloom, or so I thought. Then I looked up and saw the entire tree was in bloom. I could not believe what I was seeing! My emotions of grief and sadness turned to wonder. I ran in the house to tell my husband.

Then I went to change and return to the hospital. I got into my car and was leaving the neighborhood when my brother Jim drove into the neighborhood to my house. He had come to tell me in person our dad had just died—at the very same time I witnessed the tree in full bloom!

Everyone in the family was at dad's bedside with the exception of me, the youngest. I was not there to witness his last moments. Instead, I was presented with a special, breathtaking show, a surprise of my dad's favorite flower to comfort me in one of my most difficult hours. My worn spirit was lifted. I knew my dad was now in the presence of God. I felt peace envelop me, and in the depth of my grief, I marveled at God's mysterious ways.

Note from Susan

I had the privilege to know Kathy's father, and it is with honor I include this story. I have felt like part of their family for many, many years and think how lucky they were to have such a fun, yet spirit-filled and wonderful father. I feel privileged to have known him. When he died in 1987, he left a great void in the lives of everyone he touched. When I heard Kathy's story so long ago, I found it comforting and wonderful as well. When I decided to write this book this year, I asked her if I could share her story with others, and she was delighted to do so. Mr. James Stott, this one is for you. Gone but not forgotten. And now others will know of you as well. The light of your life truly shines among men.

All Things New
Joyce Broome
Norcross, Georgia

Another day to drag myself out of bed from my dream state—my nightmare state. I slowly open my eyes and face the hard cold truth, the unimaginable truth that our son Robby is gone from our lives forever. My husband and I are wise enough to know we will never fully recover from our loss, but we would like to be without the pain that penetrates the very depth of our souls. The earth seemed to open up and took us tumbling down within its depths when our son took his own life. We have been told this searing pain will dissipate and look forward to that time. We feel Robby's loss keenly and are aware of the hole in our hearts and the hearts of all who loved him. Some days are harder to live through than others. There are days I feel like I am going through the motions, and one day I will wake up, and all this will be a horrid dream.

One of our good neighbors and a member of the same church my husband and I attend had been doing work on our deck. One day, James called my husband and asked if he could come over and talk to both of us for a few minutes. My husband wanted to postpone it until the next day, but our friend insisted it had to be this very day. Something in his tone and behavior convinced my husband to say yes. We couldn't imagine what was so important it could not wait another day. Little did we know.

James came to our house and began his conversation by asking us what we thought of signs, wonders, and the Holy Spirit. My husband and I both agreed God can do anything, and He gave us the Bible as inspiration and history through the ages. James agreed we were all on the same page.

Continuing on, James told us just before he woke up that morning, he had a dream that was crystal clear. He saw himself on a cruise ship and the deck was filled with lots of people with party hats, colorful balloons, and streamers. Each person was singing. He said he couldn't understand the words. Next, he saw a couple wearing party hats seated at a small round table with a cake in the middle of the table. The cake was white with bright colored writing in frosting. He could not read what it said. He looked closer and recognized the couple—my husband and me. We were in tears. James remembered thinking, *God, these are my friends, and they are hurting. What can I do to help them?* He began to walk the deck of the ship while praying to God for help.

At that point, James interrupted his dream story. He recounted the movie *The Passion* and described the scene where Jesus carried the cross. His mother Mary came to him, wiped his face, and Jesus looked up at her and said, "Behold, I make all things new."

Then James continued with his dream. God said to him, "Tell them (referring to us in the dream), behold I make all things new." That was the end of the dream. Then he said, "I knew I had to let you know what I dreamt. I thought about calling and telling you over the phone, but I knew I needed to wait for both of you and tell you in person this very day. I have no clue why I'm supposed to tell you this. I only know I am. Does this have any significance to y'all?"

My husband and I just looked at each other in astonishment. He told James this very day was our son's birthday. Through our tears we smiled and said how surprising and how very personal God was even when we didn't understand His ways. I remembered the words of the gospel of Mark that states people "were amazed and astonished" at Jesus. There is so much more to Him than we could ever think or imagine. My husband and I felt comfort and peace overwhelm us. We believe He gave James this dream to let us know we are not alone in our pain. We know there will be a time when we will see our beloved son again, and our pain will cease.

Three months later from that day, our daughter announced she was pregnant. We were ecstatic. This was to be our first grandchild.

Another three months passed, and November came. November was a difficult month for us. Three years earlier on November 4, my mother died, and on the same date, my son made his first suicide attempt. Remembering all this, I felt waves of sadness crashing over me. Later in the day, something wonderful happened to lift my spirits. My pregnant daughter found out she was having a son. The due date of March 27 would be Easter Sunday this year. This little one was to be born on the day we celebrate "all things new!" I took this as a reminder to us that His ways are not our ways. He is with us always.

Note from Susan

Thank you so much for sharing this story of depth, grief, joy, and bittersweet moments. It is my hope this story will be uplifting to those who might need to hear it. I know it was not easy to share such personal pain and moments of hope. I pray that you will have the peace that passes all understanding. I remember when my friend Millie told me your little grandson was born. I know he is the light of your life. Your story touches my heart.

Goodbye, My Dear Friend
Anonymous
Orlando, Florida

I was exhausted from working late the previous night and decided to sleep in this morning. I was a young man still living at home and in that state of almost awake but not wanting to open my eyes and get up yet. Just a few more minutes of sleep before rising is my favorite part of the morning. On my stomach, with my eyes still closed, I felt a hand gently run along my back. I did not hear my bedroom door open. Thinking it was my dad trying to wake me up, I kept my eyes clamped shut and pretended to be asleep. Expecting him to say something or to hear the door to my room close after he left, I gently turned my head and peered at the door. The door was still closed, and I was alone in the room. I shut my eyes again and lay there in my comfy bed. I was puzzled, and I knew I was not dreaming.

About ten minutes later, my dad came to my room to tell me my childhood friend and one of my best buddies had just been killed in a motorcycle accident. I bolted out of bed! It wasn't my dad who had touched my back. I found out later the time he died was the same time I had this experience. It was the hand of my friend telling me goodbye.

I have heard of similar events, but nothing like this had ever happened to me. I think it is a way of letting those who are left behind know that there is much more to our lives than we can ever imagine.

I miss hanging around and confiding in my buddy a lot and think of him often. Sometimes I can't believe he is really gone. I find comfort in remembering his gentle goodbye.

Mama
Virginia Sobera
Selma, Alabama

I was married at eighteen and had my first baby when I was nineteen years old. They used forceps during this long delivery, and to this day, I wonder if this is what caused my son's severe handicap. The doctors told me that I needed to institutionalize him, and their words ripped at my heart. I could not do it. I looked at his little face, and my heart melted. I decided I would raise him at home as long as I was able to do so. He had blond hair and blue eyes and did not walk at all until he was two and a half years old. At four years old, he said only one word, *mama*. My husband was in the service, and most of the care fell to me. I was so young, and I felt like a child myself.

When my son was almost five years old, I became pregnant again. I did not know how I could take care of another child. I was exhausted. One day, my little son came down with a bad infection. Two nights later, he took a turn for the worse at eight o'clock. He burned with fever, and I was up all night caring for him by myself, and I was so afraid what was going to happen to him. A sense of powerlessness overcame me. The next day, one of my friends asked what I was doing at eight o'clock the night before. My friend had no way of knowing that was the exact time my son got sicker. I thought it unusual she would question me about that specific time.

Several days after that, my son succumbed to the illness he had been fighting so valiantly. God took him to be with Him and to raise Him. My job with him was over. I had loved him and taken care of him to the best of my ability. It made me sad to think he would never run and play with other children for his entire life. He is still in my heart, and I know I will see him again. When I do, there will be peace, happiness, and joy I cannot even imagine. God gave this little one to me for such a short time and gave me enough strength to care for him while he was here on earth. He was always innocent, he never sinned, and his struggles were different than the rest of us. It was my privilege to be his mother and feel the bond of love between mother and child that cannot be lost.

I now have two healthy, grown children, a son and a daughter. Each of them has a son and daughter, so I have been blessed again. They have been a joy in my life.

Note from Susan

I had tears in my eyes when I heard this and want to thank Virginia for sharing this story. Those of us who have children without severe problems can only imagine how difficult this must have been. Child rearing is not for the fainthearted.

Virginia's daughter, Millie, is one of my dearest friends. I met her not too long after I moved to Atlanta and had prayed to meet some great Christian women. God answered my prayer in a wonderful way. When I decided to begin writing about some of the amazing events in my life, she was the person who suggested I ask others about stories they might like to share. Her encouragement has been one of God's blessings in my life. And she has a great sense of humor.

Miracle among the Horror
Millie Ross
Orange Beach, Alabama

My two grown children and I had enjoyed a very nice Christmas in Atlanta. I heard on the news December 26, 2004, about the tsunami that had swept through several countries, including Thailand, causing untold damage and death, and I looked with horror at the news reports of devastation.

Huge waves hurled inland onto the white sandy beaches, destroying paradise beachfront towns without warning.

MORE THAN A COINCIDENCE

One of my daughter's friends, along with her family, was in Thailand for the holidays. I personally knew the mother, and the youngest daughter was a friend of my daughter. I had heard about natural disasters in the past, but now I knew someone who was involved. It was hard to wrap my feelings around this event and imagine how something like this could happen.

Not long after the news report, I heard what happened to this family. The news brought sadness, grief, joy, and amazement to my heart. As the tsunami hit that fateful day, an enormous seawall swept onto the land, covering everything in its path and then pulled everything it captured back to the sea. I was told part of my friend's family escaped by running as fast as they could to higher ground. One of the daughters and the father climbed a tree, clinging with all their might as water rushed by washing bodies and debris from the destruction with it. They were able to hold on.

Another daughter was in a villa when the back wall fell in. Water poured in, taking her and everything along with it. As this young woman was being swept away, the water took her near her father clinging in the tree. He was able to reach out and drag her to safety.

Trying to picture the destruction, the intense power of the water was so frightening. It is something I have trouble doing even now. I cannot bring myself to imagine the horror and shock everyone must have experienced.

All the family members survived with the exception of my daughter's friend. She was not able to escape the raging waters of this angry sea.

Not too long after this event, I spoke with the mother. Not knowing what to say, I conveyed my deepest sympathy. She told me she was grieved over the loss of losing her child but was grateful the rest of her family of eleven survived. Even though her heart is broken, she is thankful for what she does have. I think of her often and keep her in my prayers; I pray the peace that passes all understanding will be hers.

SUSAN FISKUM HALL

North Carolina—I Am Home
Leland Holder
Roswell, Georgia

What a rough year—I was in the process of a divorce after an eight-year marriage. As if this was not traumatic enough, my father had just died, and my mother was in poor health. Add serious financial problems, and I was in a real mess. Many people in church prayed for me to help me through this time. They knew I was struggling with grief for my parents and my marriage and the overwhelming sense of loss coupled with financial uncertainty. Being bombarded with so many unknowns and a sense of "now what?" unsettled me. I wanted to fix everything right away.

I was living in Los Angeles, California and decided to apply for a new job with a national company based there. They wanted a photographer for private country clubs, something I would enjoy doing. This was a good opportunity with a good salary, and I felt grateful for the opportunity. I was hired, went through their corporate training, and then was told the job was in a small town, Gastonia, North Carolina. *Oh great, now I have to move on top of everything else I am dealing with. From a cosmopolitan city to a small southern town—what next?* Not knowing what to do, I decided I should make the change—maybe a new start would be what I needed. I didn't think my life could get much worse.

Off I went to Gastonia, and the first thing I did was to buy the small local paper. Gastonia is a small but homey kind of town. I found an add offering a room to rent. When I called, the people told me to come right over and look at it. I decided to take the room to get settled in. When I moved in, I found the people who lived in the house smoked like chimneys. I had to put a towel under the door.

Here I was, a guy from Southern California, now living in the rural south with some real country people. And they were some of the most honest, industrious, and loving people. God had put me there for a purpose. I could not have done a better job of selecting them myself if I had tried to do so.

MORE THAN A COINCIDENCE

I was in the midst of serious depression and at times felt almost suicidal. I felt hopeless and could not see much light in my life. There didn't seem to be much point in anything—I felt like a failure.

Bur God surrounded me with the right people. They made me feel like family and cared about my troubles. They included me in family gatherings and didn't hesitate to share their great country cooking. They gave without expecting anything in return. God gave me the opportunity to experience loving your neighbors firsthand. During this time, I found a church I liked as well, and this helped me begin to feel more rooted.

All this upheaval took place in the spring of 1997. I will never forget that year. One weekend while I was especially discouraged, I drove to Black Mountain, North Carolina. I remembered spending happy times there as a child fishing, hiking, splashing near the waterfall, and playing with my friends. I drove there by myself, got out of my car, felt the chilly spring breeze on my face, walked down the path through the trees bristling with buds of new growth to the magnificent falls, and sat down on a rock by the creek. Then I did something I never do. I broke down in tears. I looked up to the sky, a glorious blue, and felt peace come over me like the comfort of home. I knew I was supposed to be in North Carolina for this period in my life, and I was not there alone.

That spring was a new beginning for me. I had passed through a time when I felt like I had fallen in a dark pit. I hated going through this time, but I learned something that is now woven into the core of me. No matter what happens in my life, I will never be alone.

I now live in Atlanta, Georgia, have my own photography business, and my life is good. In 1997, I never imagined I would be able to say such a thing. The light is shining again.

Note from Susan

Thank you for sharing this story about the valley you struggled through, a story of new beginnings. I remember you said you never declared bankruptcy, and your debts were paid off. You did your part, and God did the rest to carry you. You went through quite a few major upheavals all at the same time—major life changes. It is my hope that others experiencing similar events will ask God to be there beside them, taking them through it. Thank you for your candor in sharing your story and helping others realize it is always darkest before the dawn.

Little Samuel
Michele Pirkle
Cartersville, Georgia

In my fifth month of pregnancy, every mother's worst nightmare happened to me—I stopped feeling my baby move. When the doctor confirmed my fears, I was devastated. Adding to my grief was the fact that he made the arrangements to go through a regular labor and delivery so this baby, no longer living, could be delivered. I had no idea how I would get through this ordeal.

My husband, Keith, and I have one healthy child already, and I had one previous miscarriage. This second miscarriage was devastating for both of us. I looked at Keith, and his face was pale and drawn. During this time, my husband was so upset he quietly excused himself and went into the bathroom. The groans coming from the bathroom told me he was getting sick to his stomach from the stress. Although he didn't tell me at the time, he said he lay on the floor in the bathroom and asked for the strength to get through this ordeal so he would be able to comfort me. He wanted to be strong for me.

Our stillborn child was a boy. I lovingly cradled him in my arms and held him close to me. Both my husband and I felt waves of anguish crash over us.

I remember asking God for a name for my child, and I heard a voice say to name the child Samuel. We have no one in our family with this name. I had no idea why this name came to my mind, but I told my husband this was to be the child's name. Now I had never read the book of Samuel in the Bible and didn't know if there was such a book. Looking through my Bible, I did indeed find this chapter. It begins with Hannah praying for a son. "And she said, 'O my lord! As your soul lives, my lord, I am the woman who stood by you here, praying to the Lord. For this child I prayed, and the Lord has granted me my petition which I asked of Him. Therefore I also have lent him to the Lord; as long as he lives he shall be lent to the Lord'" (1 Samuel 1:26–28).

God granted Hannah her desire to have Samuel, and she offered him in dedication of service to the Lord as she promised. Now we knew why our child was to be named Samuel. This baby was in heaven with our Lord.

The inscription "And he grew up in the presence of the Lord." with an imprint of his tiny footprints is part of his memorial. For reasons only God knows, my husband and I were not to raise Samuel—God had other plans.

About four years later, in 2004, the Promise Keepers Conference came to Atlanta, Georgia, at the Phillips Arena. Over sixteen thousand men attended this event to hear speakers from around the country and worship God.

My husband Keith attended. Keith told me during one of the prayer times, he saw a vision of Jesus with His arms around him while he was lying down. An amazing sense of peace washed over him. It wasn't until later that Keith realized what he had been privileged to see. This vision occurred around the time that he had lain down on the floor in the bathroom and prayed for God's help. What a gift Keith received that day. God was there all the time comforting him. And what a beautiful way to give comfort to both of us in one of the lowest moments of our lives. God has also given us another healthy boy since that sad time.

God's ways are not our ways. We have, however, received many blessings and know little Samuel is with our Lord.

Note from Susan

I was honored to be a part of this 2004 Promise Keepers Conference myself—I volunteered for four days. During the conference, I remember standing from my vantage point in the back of the arena and watching thousands of men praying and worshipping God at one time. I was fortunate to be able to hear all the speakers and thought how wonderful it was for me to see God work.

I heard some amazing things had occurred during the conference. Little did I know how beautiful and personal a story I would be privileged to write, especially about someone who was in attendance.

When I heard Michele and Keith's story, it brought tears to my eyes. It still does. Thank you for sharing your story to all of us.

The Heavenly Cloud
Jim Buenahora
Marietta, Georgia

Thirty years ago was a year of a many changes and new experiences. One memory stands alone—the summer that changed some of us forever. My freshman year in high school was just beginning, and one of my classmates told our class what happened to Mike and his cousin over the summer. Very close in age and almost inseparable, Mike and his cousin had played together since they were toddlers. The classmate showed our class a photograph of a black cloud on a gray, smoky background. Then he told us the story.

After school was out one day, at the end of the previous school year, my classmate Mike and his cousin decided they would each take a camera and snap photographs of whatever they found interesting, and off they went on this adventure together. What they decided to photograph and why we still don't know. They did, however, take pictures of the same subject except for the last picture—Mike's cousin took a picture of a black cloud. Mike didn't want to waste his film on something so boring and wondered why his cousin would do such a thing. "Course, at fourteen who knows what we are thinking."

Later in the day, Mike's cousin was at home playing with his brother. They were shooting some cans with a twenty-two when Mike's cousin was accidentally shot in the head and killed. We still don't know what happened—maybe the bullet ricocheted and hit him.

Mike was devastated with this sudden, tragic loss. A couple of days later, he went to his cousin's house. He couldn't believe his cousin was gone. His aunt told him to look around his cousin's room to see if he wanted any of his cousin's belongings. He was lying on the bed in tears when he saw the camera—the same one his cousin had used on the day he died. The film was still in the camera. Mike had it developed several days later.

Mike looked at the photos, and the only photo that was different from the shots he had taken was that one last photo of a black cloud. Mike still wondered why his cousin had taken this picture and kept it in his room where he looked at it for the next few weeks.

One day, he suddenly saw something he hadn't seen beforehand and knew why his cousin had been prompted to take this photo.

In the cloud was the image of Christ. He could not see the face, but below the neck he made out the wrinkled cloak, the stigmata in His hands, even the detail of Christ's toenails. This picture made the rounds from the parish priest to the bishop and then to Rome for careful examination. I remember seeing the photo one time as a freshman and again as a senior in high school and would not have believed it if I had not seen it up close. It was authentic.

According to our classmate, Christ appeared to his cousin on the day of his death and invited him to heaven. In the midst of their grief, Christ was there for all to see.

Silent Visitors
Susan E. Hall
Atlanta, Georgia

My mother told me about an event she witnessed back in the late seventies, not too long after my father died. She was in bed listening to the radio late at night when it wavered off its station. As she looked over at the radio, she saw my father from the waist up wearing a white T-shirt and watched as he leaned over and adjusted the radio so that it picked up the station clearly. Then the image faded. She said the station did not waiver the rest of the night. I asked her if she was asleep and had dreamed this event, and she assured me that she had not.

My mother died in 1986, and about three years ago, I was visiting one of her friends who told me a similar story about her husband who had died. Rita said she was asleep in her bedroom when she heard the television come on after it had been turned off for the night. When she came to the living room, she saw her husband, and as she tried to hug him, he disappeared.

The people that are telling me these things are reliable. These are people I know, like my own mother, so I have no doubt they are seeing something of the person who died. I don't understand it. I for one think they are lucky to actually see (in some form) those who have passed on even if only for a few seconds. What is this—I have no idea—maybe it is an assurance for us.

And Your Name Is?
Anonymous
Atlanta, Georgia

I pulled into the parking lot with my mother, and as I parked the car, I felt the blood drain from my face. I almost stepped out of my car when I felt like I might pass out. I saw my husband and another woman coming out of a restaurant I had never been to before. I wanted to wipe the image from my eyes although what I saw confirmed what my gut had been telling me. *This is an evening I won't soon forget.*

My husband's actions for quite some time gave me cause for suspicion. First came the Porsche he bought, then the triathlons began for my couch potato husband, and then his clothes and behaviors began to change. I suspected midlife crisis and tried to talk with him. He was not forthright. There are just times you know someone is outright lying. It is awful. In desperation, I hired a detective that provided evidence, showing pictures of my husband with the same woman I saw on the arm of "my husband!" It looked like they were having fun. I felt consumed with rage and shock!

I had no idea he would be at this restaurant, and seeing his behavior in person is a memory that still remains in my mind. With our thirteen-year marriage, our lifestyle was comfortable, which enabled me to stay home to raise our two young children.

MORE THAN A COINCIDENCE

I needed to find out the woman's name. I needed this information for my possible divorce. I felt brokenhearted because I loved my husband and tried to keep a happy home; at least, I thought it was happy! Feeling my life crumbling around me, I went through the days like a zombie.

Not too long after the restaurant episode, my mother and I went to another restaurant for lunch. It happened again; here she was again, the same woman. This time, she was the waitress, and she waited on our table. Until that moment, I had no idea where she worked or anything about her except her picture. My heart skipped a beat. I remained calm and pretended mine was just an ordinary lunch, and I didn't snatch her eyes out. That thought may have crossed my mind. At the end of lunch, when the woman placed the check on the table, she had written, "Thanks" and her first name. My heart again skipped a beat. I was being shown what I needed. I now needed one thing, her last name. A quick phone call to the restaurant the next day, saying we had good service (no argument there) and a request for the person's last name gave me the final piece of the puzzle.

I had been praying for help with the situation. My husband was not willing to end the affair. Our marriage was over, and I felt sadness at our failure to make our relationship work. It changed my life and the lives of our two children forever.

I felt led to the information I needed without trying. Although not the answer I wanted to hear, I received the truth and the strength to muddle through a very difficult ordeal.

Oh yes, this woman was much younger than both of us. He married her, and they produced a set of twins. I figure he will be in his sixties when they graduate from high school. Just hate it when that happens!

It took me quite a long time to recover from the betrayal, and I have gone on with my life. When people tell me their divorce experiences, I tell them that they will get through it, and there is life again. It did help me with a closer walk with God when I came to the realization that He is the only one who will be with me always. Out of my experience came good in a most unexpected way.

CHAPTER 6

Surprises

Now to Him who is able to do exceedingly abundantly above all that we ask or think, according to the power that work in us. To Him be the glory in the church by Christ Jesus to all generations, forever and ever. Amen
—Ephesians 3:20–21

And Angels Do Get Their Hair Done!
Michele Pirkle
Cartersville, Georgia

With water spurting everywhere, my new beauty shop was in pandemonium. The water leak created a water park, and my children were having a great time laughing, giggling, and shrieking as they ran and slid in the water. I dissolved in tears and was glad my husband was with me as he found and cut off the water valve in the attic and stopped the water from ruining our new floors.

One of my clients walked in on this chaos. She told me that she had already driven past my new shop this evening on her way to bowl. She pulled into the bowling alley parking lot, started to remove her seat belt, and then felt she needed to turn her car around and drive the two miles back to the shop. Although this made no sense to her, she did so. She told me she knew she was supposed to come and see me. Her inner sense told her I needed some cheering up.

Everything seemed to be going wrong. I had been working for someone else in a shop for eighteen years, and my husband and I decided it was time to begin a business of our own. We would be fifty miles closer to home and our children. My husband made a serious decision to quit his salaried job to help manage the shop, and this was a step of faith for him as well. Even though I had a steady client base after eighteen years, we depended on his salary.

We are trusting we are on the right track and are going ahead with our business in faith. We know with God's help, we can be successful. I so appreciate my client who took time out of her fun evening to shower us with encouragement while we were being showered with a water leak and plenty of discouragement.

Note from Susan

I met Michele while she was working at a shop near my home. Her beautiful shop, Legends, is in the Westside Plaza Shopping Center in Carterville, Georgia. I know it will be very successful—she does a great job.

Fingerprints
Anonymous
Birmingham, Alabama

"I can't believe it!" my husband said to me and to our grown son. "As long as I have been working at the plant, nothing like this has happened to my car, and the one day I take yours!" As we all went outside to see my car, the one I lovingly take care of, my heart jumped as I saw the door on the driver's side. The paint on the car had been scraped with a metal key down to the bare metal, and the damage was very noticeable.

My husband had a management position at his company. He borrowed my newer car while his car was in the shop. We wondered if a mean-spirited employee targeted his anger at my husband or if it was just a random act of meanness. Maybe someone objected to the "right to life" sticker on the back of the car.

The next day, I did a few short errands and then decided to stop at the pool near our home to relax for a while. I was telling someone what had happened and decided to show them the damage. We approached the car on the driver's side, and the car was perfect. Knowing that I had seen the mark when I got out of the car, I walked around to look on the passenger side. There was nothing there either. Looking at the door, dumbfounded, I tried to think of any plausible reason for the damage being repaired. Could my husband have sent someone to repair the damage? That was not possible because he was not aware of my schedule that day. In addition, I was not anywhere long enough for someone to fix it, even if someone repaired the car between errands.

Knowing what my husband would say, I still called him at work. He told me he had sent no one to repair the car, so I drove home in confusion.

My son, who is in his twenties, looked at the car very carefully and found the paint was perfect. He was as amazed as I. When my husband arrived home from work, it was dark. He painstakingly inspected every inch of the car with a flashlight. There was no key mark or even a slight indentation in the paint.

I told my husband and son the only one explanation: It was a God thing! Miracles do happen every day. My son asked why God would bother to do such a thing as repair a car, and I responded that perhaps He wants us to see His power. He is showing us He is involved even in the small and unimportant events of our lives. I would say that the car did, however, have fingerprints—the fingerprints of God.

Promise Kept
Jerry Lindeman
Cumming, Georgia

I had volunteered for the Promise Keepers Conference before and wanted to be a part of this year's conference to be held in Atlanta in 2002. I have always taken leadership positions within the church and in other areas as well and know this is one of my strengths. Before I signed up via the Internet, I prayed God would find a special position to use my skills and trusted He would do just that. I then submitted my name.

When I checked to see what position I had been assigned, I was, well, shocked. For want of a better name, they made me the water boy, making sure everyone at the conference had water, soda, and ice. I spent my first day at the conference grumbling under my breath. "I am in the lowest of all positions, and I know I could do much more than this."

I was in such a rotten mood I knew I needed an attitude adjustment. I went to a dark corner staircase out of the way, got down on my knees, and gave myself up to God's services to be used where God placed me. Jesus washed the feet of the disciples, so I could do no less. I made myself a servant, and my attitude changed in seconds. My heart became cheerful. "I will do what is asked of me."

On the second day, I went about my duties, and as I delivered water to the cafeteria, I saw three of the top leaders of the conference sitting at a table. They saw me delivering water and asked my name. To my surprise, they asked if I would like a battlefield promotion. I agreed and asked what I needed to do.

In this surprising turn of events, they told me the man in charge of organizing lunch for the fifteen thousand conference attendees had not shown up. This was a serious situation—fifteen thousand hungry men and no food. Trying to contact this man by phone had proved useless, and only two hours remained until lunch. My job, if I chose to take it, was to find sixty volunteers and organize the entire operation. Thirty volunteers were in place, and sixty additional men needed to be in place in forty-five minutes. I agreed to take over. I knew this was impossible on my own, and I went to the prayer room at the conference and asked God to help me in this impossible task.

Then I returned to the volunteer check-in. I asked one of the men to help me in this challenge of finding sixty additional volunteers. Even though the man agreed, I remember thinking, *sure*; however, I continued to trust God. Over the next forty-five minutes, I focused on what I needed to do to organize the lunch so it would be served on time. As I continued to work on this, nothing happened with the volunteers until 10:45, the time they were to be in place. Just then, my helper returned with a big smile on his face. He did as I asked or, I should say, as God provided! Standing behind him was a long line of men of every size and shape.

I asked him how it happened. He told me he went out to find volunteers. One of the men he asked to help said he would be glad to do so. This man then asked how many other volunteers were needed. He was the pastor of a church, and there were fifty-nine other men in addition who could help! I had exactly the number of helpers I needed—the original thirty plus the additional sixty, and they were there at the exact time I needed them.

That day fifteen thousand men were fed lunch without any delays, and they had no idea this was no ordinary lunch.

There is even more to this story. At the end of the conference, two of the leaders asked me if I would be the event volunteer manager for the conference in 2003. I was honored to accept.

Note from Susan

Jerry felt he had a lesson not only in humility but another reminder he can always trust God even when it looks like God isn't around. Jerry was willing to do whatever he was asked, which gave him the opportunity to use his leadership skills as he had prayed. After all, God knew the luncheon would need someone with Jerry's skill set to organize the event at the last moment.

I thank Jerry for sharing this story. I was privileged to be a volunteer at the 2004 conference, and I found it was something I will always remember. From my vantage point, I was able to see sixteen thousand men listening, praying, and worshiping God in an Atlanta arena packed to capacity. I saw people with extreme dedication, working behind the scenes in an amazing way. Serving lunch to that many men at an earlier conference on short notice was a challenge to be sure. Just about impossible, but God was there. And, yes, Jerry was a part of the 2004 conference as well.

More Promises Kept
Jerry Lindaman
Cumming, Georgia

Promise Keepers is an event held once a year at large arenas in various cities in the US to help men in their walk with Christ or introduce men to a Christian way of life. I have volunteered before for Promises Keepers, and this year, I was selected as the event volunteer manager.

In the past, the event volunteer manager was provided at least thirty or forty additional tickets to the event in case there was a serious need for free tickets. This year, I was told there would be no free tickets at this conference. I was surprised, and I confirmed this information with one of the coordinators.

On the second day of the event, I helped near the retail tent where books and tapes from the conference were on sale. This area was filled with people—there must have been at least seventy-five or so conference attendees and volunteers. All tickets were sold out—

the arena holds over fifteen thousand people. From out of the crowd, a man walked up to me, saw my volunteer badge, and told me he had an extra ticket. He wondered if I knew someone who might need it. I told him there was no need at the present; however, I would keep it in case the opportunity arose.

Putting it in my pocket, I was heading back to the volunteer area and talking with some friends when a call came in on my radio telling me a pastor at the conference brought a young man with him. You guessed it—he needed one ticket. This young man had never been to a Promise Keepers Conference, and the pastor thought this conference might be just what he needed. I told this young man Jesus had given me his ticket just an hour ago. That was the only request for a free ticket I received during the entire conference. I guess I shouldn't be surprised. God provided exactly what was needed at just the right time.

Next Time I Won't Use the Phone
Susan E. Hall
Atlanta, Georgia

As I was dashing out of the house for an appointment, I heard my home phone ring. I was in a hurry and saw it was my friend's home number. I decided I would call her when I returned home so I would not be late for my appointment.

I had written down the directions for this appointment; however, I had not written the complete street name for the exit. I was sure I could find where I was going. Then I realized I was lost. When I couldn't find the correct street, I knew I was going to be late or not make my appointment at all.

I used my cell phone to call the person I was meeting for directions but got voice mail. Next, I tried to call my friend (who had called right before I left) on her home phone because she knew exactly how to get where I was going. Her voice mail answered. I was thinking I did not want to miss the appointment, but it looked like that was what was going to happen. At that moment, my friend called me on my cell phone. I thought she had heard my message on her home phone just a minute ago and was returning my call. She didn't know I had just called her and was calling me from her cell phone. Needless to say, she gave me directions, and I made my appointment on time. Sometimes I think these situations are God moments for me to realize He is always with us even in the smallest of details.

The Peace Lily
Anonymous
Atlanta, Georgia

I think about my mother often, and her passing in 1994 is still on my mind. I miss her lot. Of the fourteen brothers and sisters, I was the one who stayed near our mother longer than any of the others. When I married at twenty-five, I lived only seventeen miles away. We were very close and were able to spend lots of time together.

It was only a few days after my mother's death. My husband and I liked to eat in the dining room; however, this time, we decided we would eat in the living room. As I sat eating dinner and staring at the meat on my plate, something out of the corner of my eye caught my attention. I had placed a beautiful white peace lily in full bloom on the floor. This vase had been at my mother's funeral service. I did a double take when I saw one of its leaves moving. As the leaf bobbed up and down, I saw my mother's transparent smile. I have never in my life seen anything like this. I cried out to my husband. As soon as he looked up and saw the leaf moving, it stopped. We leaped from our chairs to see if there was anything in the room causing a draft, but there were no fans, no air vents blowing, nothing.

Not believing what we had seen, I dashed to the phone to call my oldest brother and let him know what happened. After I finished my feeble attempt to explain what my husband and I had just seen, he proceeded to tell me about some family business related to my mother's estate. He told me the timber from our mother's property was about to be sold. I had not known about this, and he was quite surprised one of my sisters had not told me.

I took this as a sign I am being protected and Someone is still watching over me. If I hadn't had this once-in-a-lifetime experience with the peace lily and my mother's smile appearing, I would not have called my brother. I wouldn't have known about the sale that soon. Because of legal involvement, I would have found out eventually; however, it was beneficial that I knew when I did. I needed to be involved. My sister eventually informed me. They say God works in mysterious ways. This is one for the books!

Perfect Timing
Susan E. Hall
Atlanta, Georgia

I lived in Orlando, Florida, in the early nineties as a single parent raising my youngest son Brian. My oldest son, Spence, was in college, and my middle son, Brett, was living with his father. Brian decided he wanted to live with his father when his eighth-grade class ended. As much as I wanted him to stay with me, we allowed him to make the decision which parent to live with. This was very difficult for me, and I wanted very much for him to stay. I would miss him more than he would ever know. There are times in life when there are no easy solutions.

It was during this time that Spence graduated from Florida State University and decided he would live with us while he was looking for a job. I was thrilled to have him around again, and it was nice for his youngest brother as well.

Spence was job-hunting during this time, but nothing feasible presented itself. He continued looking for about six months, and I remember saying perhaps he would find a job at the same time Brian was going to be moving out. As it turned out, Spence found a new job out of town. This job began the day after Brian's last day of school—the day he was moving out. Yes, they both left the same day. I found this timing amazing.

It was difficult to let them go, but I remembered how God let me have both of them together for such a time. In my sadness, I was thankful. I know this was not a coincidence. I remember my mother told me several times children are God's gifts to us. We have them for such a short time to love and raise. I have always been thankful for my time with all three of them.

Although my time of raising them was over sooner than I wanted, the fact that they would both leave the same day with no planning on their own was just another reminder to me that God's timing is sometimes just astonishing.

Prodigal Daughter
Anonymous
Atlanta, Georgia

Anyone who has ever had children can relate to the fact that even though we do our best to raise them, there are times that are so difficult we don't know what to do. Meet our daughter Maria (name changed), the poster child for difficult teenagers. She was difficult from the age of twelve until about twenty. Problems—name some! Alcohol, anger, rebellion, a time in drug rehabilitation, and every day was a trial. Thinking it might be easier when she graduated from high school, we enrolled her at the University of Georgia near our home. The fact that she never bothered to show up and dropped out of school was not a promising sign that things were going to improve. My husband and I were disappointed and furious with her. We were at our wit's end.

About this time, I decided to go on a spiritual retreat known as a cursillo. The retreat encompasses a weekend and is common in most of the Methodist, Baptist, Episcopal, and Catholic churches. I have been to one before and find it a wonderful spiritual respite. This time, I attended as one of the instructors. One of my friends was struggling through a difficult divorce (What divorce isn't?), and she was brimming with anger. I thought this retreat might help her deal with some of her anger, and she agreed to attend with me. I was delighted.

During one of the church services, we could see the huge cross on the altar. Part of the service involves inviting people to come and use an actual hammer and nail to symbolically nail their sins to the cross. I was thinking I could help my friend with her pain, but God used this time to work on me. I came to the realization I was filled with bottled up anger at my daughter for all the challenges through all the years. I surprised myself as I went to the foot of the cross and symbolically nailed my anger to the cross and asked Jesus to help me. Instantly, I felt as if a great burden lifted from me.

Upon returning home, I wrote a four-page letter to my daughter and asked for her forgiveness for my anger. My daughter had not been speaking to me, and it warmed my heart when she called me several days later and told me all was okay, and I was forgiven. We both made a promise to each other not to bring up the past.

After this experience, our relationship changed, and we now have a wonderful time together. My daughter doesn't go to any organized church at this point. She surprised her father and me not long ago by calling her dad to ask if he would help her in Bible study. She told him he was the only one she would trust with that subject. My husband is a man of honor. She chose well.

After being married for seven years, Maria and her husband had their first child. They let us take our little grandchild to church on Sundays. I get tears in my eyes when I think of how far we have come, and know I have been blessed abundantly, and I am expecting many more blessings. Could it be that since my daughter has her own daughter, we will both continue to get closer in our relationship? That is my prayer.

The Crowning Glory
Peggy Gentner
Atlanta, Georgia

After many months of treatment for breast cancer, with my hair falling out in clumps from the treatment, I made a decision on April 12, 1999. I decided I would shave my head and wear a wig until my hair grew in. I despised this idea, but after struggling with fear, anger, and discouragement, and just about everything else you might imagine, I decided I was glad to be alive. This was just a temporary event in my life.

MORE THAN A COINCIDENCE

My sister, Patty, came from Florida to participate in this "beauty event" with me. Now, if you are going to do anything that takes lots of encouragement, my sister Patty is the one you want with you. She has a great sense of humor and can turn the worst situation into something to make you laugh. Yes, even this. Now, no woman wants to be bald. After all, most of us spend a lot of time on our hair. With Patty as the "beautician," we did it, and soon all my dark brown was all over the bathroom floor—every last strand.

When my hair grew back in, I decided I would now become a blonde. After all, blondes do have more fun.

Just a few weeks ago, in April 2005, I started moving from Atlanta to Naples. In the midst of packing my things, I was cleaning out my dresser and found an envelope. Inside was a lock of hair I had saved the day I shaved my hair off. And the day I opened the envelope—April 12, 2005—was exactly five years to the day. I knew that was not a coincidence but a reassurance and a reminder for me of how things had turned around. I had come through a difficult time and am now blessed with good health. Somehow I know God is with me no matter what happens in my life.

Note from Susan

This traumatic event reminds me how amazing my friend is. I have known Peggy since we were both fifteen and both cheerleaders. Peggy was the captain, homecoming queen, on the honor roll—well, you get the picture. On top of all of this, she is and has always been like a ray of sunshine around those who are fortunate to cross her path. I am delighted to say that Peggy is now fine—she is healthy, and she continues to sparkle among us, as a blonde no less. And her blonde hair now is her crowning glory!

I had not reconnected with her when she was going through her treatments. Please read "Priceless Without Measure" to find out how we "happened" to bump into one another again and reconnect our friendship in 2003.

SUSAN FISKUM HALL

The Painful Truth
Anonymous
Lake Mary, Florida

My husband and I had been married for about fifteen happy years, and we had two children, a boy and a girl. I began to have serious medical problems, and after many office visits, the doctor told me I required major surgery. The procedure to correct my condition resulted from severe nerve damage, and I suffered continuous pain, day in and day out. The pain medication helped somewhat, but I felt miserable. Six surgeries followed one after the other to no avail. I did my best, but most days were difficult. This was a taxing time for both of us.

During this challenging time, my husband seemed to "forget" the wedding vow he pledged of being there in sickness and in health. Having an affair seemed to be his solution, and if that wasn't bad enough, he became involved with my "best friend." Or at least, I thought she was. When I found about the affair, I experienced feelings of rejection, anger, sadness, rage. I had them all, sometimes all at the same time. The physical pain I had been suffering combined with the emotional pain combined to make this one of the most agonizing experiences of my life. I felt desolate and alone except for my wonderful sister and some friends who were there for me. I don't know what I would have done without them.

My husband and I worked hard to save the marriage. We had many discussions, and he answered my questions. I told him I still loved him and forgave him and would not bring the subject up again. I wanted our marriage to work. I did tell him that if he had another affair, our marriage would be over. Trust is integral to a good marital relationship. True to my word, I never brought up the incident in the next two-year period, and I did forgive him.

My seventh surgery was scheduled, and when I awoke from anesthesia, my pain was gone. Finally things were looking up. The recovery period for this surgery was about six weeks, and two weeks after, I began to suspect my husband had reverted to his former behavior and was having another affair. I did not want to accuse him until I had proof, but his behavior was suspicious. I prayed for the truth beyond any doubt and the strength to withstand whatever it was. For the next three months, I did not bring up anything about my suspicions and continued as if everything was normal. Then, one day, our children and I were driving home from church, and I felt directed by God to look in my husband's car. I knew I needed to search the car, something I have never done.

As we pulled up in the driveway, I told the children to go into the house and change into their play clothes. With a high level of anxiety, I went to my husband's car, unlocked it, and saw some Valentine wrapping paper on the car seat. I had received flowers with no wrapping paper, so it had nothing to do with any gift for me. I decided to open the glove compartment—I felt uncomfortable doing all this, but again, I felt directed to do so. I could feel myself almost shaking, and my heart was pounding so loud I could hear it. What I saw made my heart drop. I found letters from a woman professing undying love for my husband. Seeing love notes and pictures of her was a real showstopper as well! It got worse. Opening up a checkbook from an unknown bank showed large amounts of cash deposits in this bank in his name only. I had no idea we (or I should say he) had any money except what was in our joint accounts.

It took all the strength I could muster to walk in shock into our home and into the bedroom. As my husband slept, I threw the envelope and love notes at him. I yelled at him and told him that was it—our marriage was over. With this declaration came great pain—pain at ending a seventeen-year marriage and one that had been relatively happy until I became so sick several years ago. I had tried everything I could to stay married, but at this point, there was no room for reconciliation. It does take two people.

The next year, I struggled with more emotions than ever before. For the first time, I understood and was consumed with rage toward my ex-best friend. I had a difficult time functioning, but I continued to work and take care of my children.

One day at work, I received an unsigned typewritten letter that said it was from this ex-friend, asking for forgiveness. I do not know if she or someone in my office who is a friend of hers wrote it. While

I read the words, I felt as if God whispered in my ear to remind me how He forgives us. It was not long after that I laid my hatred at the cross of Jesus, and my hatred left me! I forgave my ex-husband and my ex-best friend. It is true the hate we carry hurts us—the other person may or may not be sorry. They are usually not thinking about us or the pain they caused. We are commanded to forgive as Christ forgave us, and as difficult as that is, we are the ones set free.

Now years later, ex-husband and I are friendly and attend many functions in our children's lives. God is the one who took away my hatred and healed me. I could not do this on my own. God gave me the strength to go through something I never wanted to happen and never thought I would be able to survive. He led me to the truth, and the truth set me free!

What Brand Is This?
Susan E. Hall
Atlanta, Georgia

Many years ago, in the early seventies, when my oldest son, Spence, was about three years old and the only child at that time, the two of us were visiting my mother and father in Orlando, Florida. This was about a two-hour trip from our home in Dade City, Florida. Spence is not going to be thrilled with me writing this story—I can see him rolling his eyes—but he is the star of the story. I am sure he will forgive me. Besides, I am the author and his mother. Must keep him on his toes.

We had a great time on our visit as usual. Spence was adorable and always laughing as both my mother and father would attest to. He was the first grandchild, and they were crazy about him.

At the end of our visit, I was packing the car with all our paraphernalia. I had no idea how much stuff one child needed until Spence was born. As I was ready to close the trunk, my mother handed me a roll of toilet paper and insisted I put it in the trunk with everything else. This was before disposable cloths were on the market. Since this was a highly unusual thing for her to do, I asked her why she gave it to me. She just said to take it, so I added it to everything else in the trunk and forgot about it.

We had been in the car for over an hour and came upon a long stretch of highway with miles and miles of vacant land—no gas stations, restaurants, nothing. Well, you guessed it—somehow my mother knew just what a three-year-old was going to need. We had to stop in the middle of nowhere.

I thought about the numerous times we made that drive before and after that visit. Never before or after did my mother hand me a roll of toilet paper, and we never needed it any other time. Something prompted her to help us before we even knew we needed help. There were so many times my mother just seemed to know things that would be unexplainable. I take these things as a reminder that God is with us even in the minute details of our lives. And sometimes we need to listen to these nudges.

You Just Never Know
Susan E. Hall
Atlanta, Georgia

My brother was at work in Orlando in August 2005. Part of his job required field work looking at properties for Orange County in Orlando, Florida. David was in the outskirts of Orlando, and as he left a property he was working on that day, he drove back to the main road. A few minutes later, he realized he had not taken a photo of the property for his records, so he turned around and returned to the property. This only took a few minutes, so he took the photo and again returned immediately to the main road. This time, there was something different that caught his attention—he noticed a car on the median on this major highway. The driver of the car had opened the car door, and although he was still in the car, his feet were on the grass, and his head was a little down. My brother was thinking he looked odd and wondered if the man was sick. He did not look up and see my brother.

What is amazing about this story is the fact that my brother did not stop. I have the greatest brother in the world, if I do say so myself, and he is always helping people. He carries a medical emergency bag in the car and has emergency training. If someone needs help, he is the man.

My brother said he decided if he saw any policemen on the highway, he would stop and tell them about the car because something just didn't seem quite right. He didn't see any policemen and did not call 911, as it didn't seem to be an emergency.

That evening, as he watched the news, a reporter talked about a man who stabbed his fiancée numerous times and then killed her with a samurai sword. The man then ran outside and took off by car. Bad luck for him, he had car trouble. The man later turned himself in. This was the man my brother saw in the median that day. What made my brother go against his natural helping instincts could only be God's protection—the helping hand we don't even realize is there.

More Voices
Jill South
Dacula, Georgia

I was in high school and seventeen years old when the girl who was valedictorian of our class sent me a photo for the yearbook project we were working on. I remember she said to me, "I don't know if we will ever survive those yearbook deadlines." A thought popped into my head that I would, but she would not. This made no sense to me, and I thought it ridiculous. After all, this girl had a full scholarship to the school of medicine in St. Louis, Missouri. I was stunned when she was killed two and a half weeks later, in June 1970. A drunk driver going the wrong way on I-75 right above Cincinnati, Ohio, ended her life. What a waste! I remember my thoughts several weeks before about her death and thought it must be a coincidence.

The following summer, my sister and I were visiting my grandmother in Fort Lauderdale, Florida, and we had a great time. It was August 1971. It was with sadness we got on the plane to return home. I remember seeing my grandmother outside the plane, waving goodbye to us. Then it happened again. This time, I heard an audible voice very distinctly tell me I would never see our grandmother alive again. When I told my sister, we both dissolved in tears. I hoped my voice was not correct.

That fall, I went off with excitement to begin my freshman year in college. On March 1 of the next year, I was told my grandmother had cancer and had only three months left to live. I was devastated. I called the airlines right away to make a reservation to see her on my spring break. My flight was for March 10. On March 4, my grandmother died without knowing she had cancer. I never did see her again. I began to think it was about time I take the voices I heard as fact.

Years later, in February 1993, my father suffered a stroke. I heard the voice again while I was at the hospital. This time, it was good news that my father would live for another four years. Because he was in such poor condition at the hospital, the doctors and nurses gave up on him and were just about to let him die. It took some screaming on my part to get their attention so they would pay attention and help him. He lived another four years and nine months and improved enough to have a pretty good life. He was happy every day, and I consider that extra time with him a gift.

Something interesting happened again. Two weeks after my father had his stroke, I heard an audible voice say, "he will not make it to his next birthday." I was sitting on the couch, and no one was in the room. I said out loud, "who won't?" thinking the voice was talking about my father who suffered the stroke several weeks ago. The voice said it was referring to my grandfather. Now my grandfather had been in marvelous health his entire life, was eighty-nine years old, still drove, and took care of himself. He had just been diagnosed with bone cancer. He was getting ready to move in with my mother at the end of February 1993. His birthday was May 16. True to the warning I received, he passed away April 2 and did not live to celebrate another birthday.

I hate having these warnings because they are always right. The voice is a man's audible voice. One thing I will say—it gives me time to try to prepare and say goodbye, and when I hear these warnings, I now heed them. The warnings are always about health or life-and-death issues.

I remember my mother told me that when my father was about eight or nine years old, he told his mother that his grandmother had just died. She asked him where he ever got such an idea and told him he was wrong. Just minutes later, the phone rang with the news confirming what he had just told his mother had come to pass. Guess this "gift" of the audible voice runs in the family.

Instincts could only be God's protection—the helping hand we don't even realize is there.

NOTES

SUSAN FISKUM HALL

MORE THAN A COINCIDENCE

SUSAN FISKUM HALL

MORE THAN A COINCIDENCE

ABOUT THE AUTHOR

Susan Elizabeth Fiskum Hall is a Florida native who grew up in Orlando, Florida, graduated from Bishop Moore Catholic High School, raised her three sons Spence, Brett, and Brian Winn in Dade City as a stay-at-home mom before acquiring her real estate broker license. After moving back to Orlando, she also completed her bachelor of science degree from Florida Southern College. Graduating Cum Laude, she likes to remind anyone who is considering not returning to school because they are older that it was over twenty years from that first class until she walked across the auditorium at the Florida Southern College campus to receive her degree. Susan worked full-time while continuing to pursue her degree. It is never too late.

After working in real estate for about five years, she made a change and worked for a global company as a major account representative. When they wanted to relocate her to Atlanta, always relying on God's direction, she sure did not want to move. Asking

God to make it very clear if she was to move and telling Him all the reasons why that would *not* be a good idea, God had other ideas. Figuring it was safe that it might not happen for years since she didn't have to move until her house was sold, she was pretty sure that she would not be moving any time soon. The first people to look at the house made an offer in seventeen days, did not care when she moved out, and gave her the asking price. She closed August 1 and exactly one year later was closing on her Atlanta home. Although this was a major and frightening move to such a large, unknown city and state, He made it a perfect move. Talk about taking on new territory! Her oldest son, Spence, had moved from Florida to Atlanta about five months before to work on acquiring his master's degree from Emory University while he worked full-time. She said evidently God sent him first to this brand-new land, which was a blessing in itself. She has now become a Georgia Peach.

Life went on, and through some transitions, Susan began a career in a well-known bank as a relationship banker for thirteen years. When God made it clear it was time to retire from banking, she knew it was time to publish this book. So from fifteen years when she began collecting stories until now, she is delighted to have this chance to finally share these stories, and she is hoping they will be enjoyed by many. Susan resides in Atlanta, Georgia, and delightfully enjoys having three adorable grandsons: Lucas, Phoenix, and Hunter. Spence and his adorable fiancée Emily live in Atlanta, and Brett and Monica, my beautiful daughter-in-law, and those grandchildren live in Coral Gables, Florida, and Brian Winn is in Miami, Florida.

Susan Elizabeth Fiskum Hall

Donated by Prison Alliance
Write us a letter & enroll in
our PA Bible Study today!
PO Box 97095 Raleigh NC 27624